BOLDLY GO

Center Point
Large Print

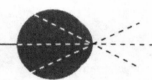

**This Large Print Book carries the
Seal of Approval of N.A.V.H.**

BOLDLY GO

REFLECTIONS ON A LIFE
OF AWE AND WONDER

WILLIAM SHATNER
WITH JOSHUA BRANDON

CENTER POINT LARGE PRINT
THORNDIKE, MAINE

This Center Point Large Print edition
is published in the year 2022 by arrangement with
Atria Books, a division of Simon & Schuster, Inc.

Grateful acknowledgment is made for permission
to quote from the lyrics of "What Do We Know"
by Robert Sharenow and William Shatner.

The text of this Large Print edition is unabridged.
In other aspects, this book may vary
from the original edition.
Printed in the United States of America
on permanent paper sourced using
environmentally responsible foresting methods.
Set in 16-point Times New Roman type.

ISBN: 978-1-63808-510-2

The Library of Congress has cataloged this record
under Library of Congress Control Number: 2022942093

My family—which includes my daughters, my sons-in-law, and grandchildren—has a new member. His name is Clive. Clive is a step into the future. Unbeknownst to him, the world is changing rapidly. The recipient of all those changes will be Clive. This book is dedicated to the Clives of the world, who are being born into a maelstrom of activity. If we are diligent enough given all the new, wonderful things that are being invented even as you read this book, the world as we know it may continue to exist. That will be up to Clive and company. I wish them well.

The cosmos is also within us.
We're made of star-stuff.
We are a way for the universe
to know itself.
—Carl Sagan

CONTENTS

INTRODUCTION

Knowledge feeds me. It's as necessary to my existence as oxygen. It thrills me.

Long before Gene Roddenberry put me on a starship to explore the galaxy, long before I actually ventured into space, I had been gripped by my own search for knowledge, for even a fraction more understanding than I'd had before. Perhaps, even more, for *meaning.* If I never succeed, never discover the answer to the age-old question of *why,* to be always learning, always wondering . . . well, the quest itself keeps me vital. I get a tingle down my spine when I'm presented with an opportunity to learn something new, a daily occurrence for me, even at ninety-one years old. Open your eyes, your ears, your mind, and you'll quickly be overcome by the wonder that surrounds us. I am never so thrilled as when the word *wow* escapes my mouth. It's an almost involuntary expression of childlike delight at learning something new. I probably say *wow* more now than when I was a child, and I am absolutely enchanted by that fact.

These *wow* feelings are not all intellectual. I could sit at home reading, hour after hour, immersed in knowledge, but that's not enough.

To me, experiences must be felt. They must be lived. We need to reach out for love as well as fear if we want to stay vibrant.

Shortly after my ninetieth birthday, I went swimming with sharks—in the most dangerous and frightening of ways. I was invited to be a featured guest on an episode of *Shark Week*. My philosophy has long been to say yes to new possibilities. The adage that you'll regret the things you didn't do may be a cliché, but I really believe it, so I strive to answer the phone when opportunity calls. Soon after accepting the offer, I found myself on a boat, ready to go into the water with fifteen-foot tiger sharks—some of the most ferocious beings in the ocean, second only to the great white.

The dive organizers had dressed me in a wet suit, complete with scuba gear. I had dived many times in my life, so I was familiar with the accoutrements, but my previous experience could not have prepared me for what lay ahead, and what lay beneath. The guides threw ground bait (or *chum*) out onto the surface of the water to attract the fish they were looking for. In this case, sharks. Right away, we succeeded in enticing some smaller sharks to the surface.

"There are two difficult points in this exercise," announced our Bahamian guide, Neal Watson. "Going into the water, and coming out. Because all of these sharks on top of the water are looking for chum, and if they think you're their chum, they might bite your ass."

Great. These chummers are not really my "chums" in the traditional sense, I thought.

"You take the same risk getting out of the water, because the last thing to disappear out of the water is your ass, so they might want to take a bite out of that."

Wonderful. I dropped down into the water and sank forty feet to the ocean floor. Right in front of me were four massive tiger sharks. Suddenly, being on the surface with my "chums" didn't seem so bad. Neal came down with us, and I felt a modicum of comfort knowing he'd spent his whole life doing this. He was a real pro.

Then again, my brain chimed in, *things only have to go wrong once.*

In front of us, one of the handlers fed the sharks to keep them in the area (it's better TV if they don't swim away). I watched as each shark made a beeline for the handler, who would pull out of the way at just the last minute, allowing the shark to grab its food and pass by.

I sat down on a rock in the sand, watching with awe and a great deal of fear as these massive creatures swam around me. When they opened their mouths, the sharks appeared to have fangs that looked like something out of a horror movie. One of the handlers had positioned himself behind me, and later explained he did so because

11

tiger sharks are ambush predators, who like to circle around and get you from behind. He literally "had my back" to prevent an attack from the rear. *Fantastic.*

At one point, the tiger sharks started coming toward us, taking particular interest in one of our cameramen. One moved at him like a charging dog. I was able to think only two things in that moment. First, *At least the shark isn't charging toward me!* And second, *What the hell am I* doing *down here at ninety years of age swimming with sharks? Why on earth am I* doing *this?!*

The best answer I can come up with is that I don't know how *not* to be doing. I really would regret not giving myself a chance to experience something new and to learn in the process. I've spent my entire life taking what seem to be unnecessary risks. I've done things that should have killed me. I've been skydiving, even though I'm afraid of heights; I literally screamed all the way down. My fear of doing it was very real, but my fear of *not* doing it was worse. It's as if I have an inverted instinct for danger. My mind doesn't run screaming away from it; it somehow forces me to run *toward* danger.

Years ago I was making a film called *Disaster on the Coastliner*, starring Lloyd Bridges, Raymond Burr, and other heroic actors of the age. We were shooting on a deserted Connecticut rail line, which we were using for a big action sequence with a moving train. (You didn't think I was going to give you the whole shark story up front, did you? I'm an actor; we have to create suspense!)

In *Disaster on the Coastliner*, my character had to run across the top of the train, making a mad dash across to the engine compartment to rescue Paul L. Smith's character, all the while being pursued by a helicopter. This was clearly going to be a hell of a stunt.

I asked the director, Richard C. Sarafian, "How are you going to shoot this?"

He said the stuntman would do it in the wide shot, then he walked over to check the camera setup. Okay, but I really wanted to know how he was going to do the *close-up*.

I watched the stuntman, and I can tell you, this was one brave guy. The train was going about forty miles per hour, and he was bent over against the wind. Now, I'm a pilot, so I could tell that the stuntman was creating an airfoil—the wind coming at him was lifting him slightly off the surface of the engine. It's not dissimilar to flying a single-engine Cessna 150; once you're going about thirty to forty miles per hour, you already start to get lift. It must have been terrifying for the stuntman—he was basically a light aircraft at this point, with none of the controls!

They got the shot and it looked terrific.

Now I said to the director, "Okay, how are you going to shoot *me* in this scene?"

He wasn't sure. "Background projection, most likely," he decided, which meant going back to the studio, building a train rig, and simulating the effects of it moving with lights, wind machines, and other Hollywood gimmickry.

This is where my inverted instincts suddenly kicked in. "Well, you know," I said, "I can get on top of that thing, if you want."

The director's eyes lit up. "You can?"

"Sure!" I exclaimed with undue confidence. "How fast is it going to go?"

"Well, it doesn't have to go faster than ten miles per hour."

"I'll do it. I'll get on top of the moving train."

So, there I went. Up on top of this loco-motive—a *Diesel*. It's important that you know that it's a Diesel, since those things are built in such an aerodynamic way that there are no pro-trusions on the curved surface of the cars. There is nothing to tie cables to, so there were no cables attached to me. I was up there completely alone. No harness. No net. Let's face it, *no brain*. Frankly, I can't believe they let me do this. There is no way this would happen today, whether I'm William Shatner or William Jones. It just isn't done. But back in Connecticut in 1979 with a crazy ambitious director and my own inverted instincts for danger, there I was.

The train started up, the helicopters—one to chase me, the other one to *film* the first one chasing me—rose into the air, and we did the scene. I was running across the train like my life depended on it (it did), giving my absolute all as an actor to this scene and this thoroughly ill-advised stunt.

We finished the scene; the train came back to the starting point; I climbed down and walked over to the director.

"How was it?" I asked eagerly.

"It was great. It was terrific," he said.

There's no greater feeling as an actor than when the director tells you that you've done a good job. You live for that feeling, that validation, knowing that in your continued pursuit of perfecting your craft, the work you do will—

But there was something amiss. A look in the director's eye.

"What is it?" I asked, foolishly.

He hesitated. "Well . . ." he began to reply.

Well. It's just like *but.* You know the rest of that sentence isn't going to be good. You know your days of running across a moving train haven't ended.

"It looked like the train was going at ten miles per hour. And if we speed up the film too much, it'll just look goofy."

Again, those anti-instincts kicked in.

"Let's do it faster," I suggested.

I got back on the train; they took it up to twenty miles per hour. I did the whole thing again, twice as fast. Twice as scary. We finished the scene and I climbed back down.

"How was that?" I asked breathlessly.

"It was great. It was terrific. You were incredible!"

I was thrilled, the exhilaration of a job well done reverberating through my body. This was why I'd acted; this was why I had devoted my life to my craft, to—

That look again on the director's face.

"What?"

"Well . . . it looked like you were going twenty miles per hour."

I eventually did the stunt at the full forty miles per hour like the stuntman, running across the train, under a bridge, around a curve, two helicopters following. I even had to stand up and reach for one of the helicopters at the end, so they could cut to the wide shot of the stuntman climbing into the helicopter to escape certain death on top of that train from hell.

When the stunt was over, I thought, *This was the most incredibly stupid, idiotic thing I could have done.*

Which brings me back to those sharks.

They made a beeline for the cameraman. Was he going to capture his own mauling on film?

No, it wouldn't seem so. Neal calmly moved the sharks aside; he knew just how to guide them. These were enormous, dangerous creatures with fangs, and he just moved them over. It was an incredible thing to behold.

We were also accompanied by Cristina Zenato, a lady we affectionately called the "shark whisperer." Cristina was so in tune with the sharks that she could command them to obey her, in a way. She had first gone to the Bahamas as a tourist almost thirty years earlier and found her calling. She stayed and became a shark expert.

Cristina showed us how she could put the sharks into what is termed *tonic immobility* (or "tonic shock")—a peculiar quirk whose reason for existing in nature I don't entirely understand. Essentially, Cristina could turn a shark upside down and stroke its belly, causing it to lapse into a strange hypnotic sleep. Apparently, orcas use this technique to turn great whites upside down, pet their bellies until they are in this trance, and then eat their livers. Some birds have a similar impulse: if you put them on their backs and stroke them, they're immobilized, often out of fear that a predator is going to eat them, making their best bet to stay still and play dead.

Cristina guided one of these immense creatures over to me; it was so docile under her command that she put it on my lap. *(I've got a shark on my lap! What the hell am I doing here?!)*

I found myself petting this beautiful being. The rest of the crew were wearing chain mail–type suits, but for some reason they'd figured I didn't need one, so I was able to feel the quality of the shark's skin and touch its fins. Then, I inadvertently put a finger near its gills, and *bam!*—it swam off. It wasn't immobilized; it could have chosen to take a bite out of me, if it had wanted to.

About ten minutes later, Cristina coaxed another shark over and I stroked this one as well. Perhaps it was immobilized by fear, but I prefer to think it was mesmerized by love. By touch. By a deeper connection that I can't explain. I believe with all my soul that it's there.

In that moment, stroking the belly of this shark, whose skin felt like a strange, rough carpet, my fear disappeared. I remembered what the hell I was doing there. I was learning. I was communicating. I know in my heart that these sharks could tell I was not a threat, and they responded with love.

When it came time to return to the boat, I wound my way up through the multitude of sharks, while the smaller ones were still chumming overhead. As I got above the surface and safely out of reach—my derriere the last piece of me to disappear out of the water—I could have sworn I heard one of the sharks say to another, "Get a load of that asshole."

It was an incredible, frightening, wonderful experience. You could say I haven't learned my lesson. Or you could say I've learned a different lesson. Dare I say a better lesson? For me, perhaps. Let's be clear: I'm not advocating for you, dear reader, to go swimming with sharks or run across moving trains without a safety harness. The lawyers would like me to make that clear. We want you to stay nice and safe—and to buy more of my books. Have you read *Shatner Rules*?

We are often reminded to stop and smell the roses. I have to go further. Stop and smell *everything*. Smell the roses, smell the grass, smell the weeds.

Wait . . . Shatner wants me to smell the weeds?! That's how I'm supposed to live? Well, I'm ninety-one years old; how old are you?

My point is that there is beauty all around us, and there is something ineffable about taking it all in—including the weeds—especially when you stand back to contemplate that those weeds are made of the exact same "star stuff" as we are, as Carl Sagan so famously put it once. The weeds in the ground, the air we breathe, the animals with whom we share bonds, the stars in the sky . . . they're all made of the same atoms, and they're likely all connected in ways we can't even yet imagine. Honestly, just *thinking* about that gives me chills. How can your body not want to keep you alive for as long as possible when all these opportunities exist for you to behold on a daily basis?

If you allow yourself to be awed by life, to keep drinking in its limitless knowledge, to keep striving for answers, to enjoy the beauty around us at every moment, to never stagnate . . . well, then you might find yourself living for a very long time, and ideally, prospering. Or in the absence of the longevity and self-defined prosperity you seek, you might well find meaning, or even better, happiness.

— CHAPTER 1 —

WE BELONG TOGETHER

I heard a story once about a young John Lennon. In his school days, a teacher supposedly asked the class the question, "What do you want to be when you grow up?" The teacher was likely expecting the usual range of answers: a doctor, a lawyer, an astronaut, or even, heaven forbid, an actor. But ever precocious, young Johnny is said to have replied, "Happy." The teacher told him he hadn't understood the assignment; according to Lennon, he replied that the teacher didn't understand life.

What makes us happy, or sets up the conditions for us to be able to experience contentment? What allows us to form connections with each other and the world around us? These are questions that have fascinated me for a long time. I truly believe that we are bound to each other and to the fabric of the universe, down to the microbe, down to the atom, and everything contained therein. We see evidence of it every day. If one species is displaced from our delicately balanced ecosystem, there will be damage to the whole planet. If essential connections between human beings are disrupted, damage to those human beings will occur on every level.

At our most fundamental, we exhibit an essential aloneness. We begin alone in the womb; as we emerge, we are alone until gathered up by, ideally, loving people who constitute, in most cases, our immediate families, and we are bonded to them. We then go through life testing the strength of those bonds, through distance, disagreements, diverging interests. Each of those tests can have the effect of allowing that essential aloneness to resurface. Between our births and our inevitable deaths—both events we will experience alone—we try to fill those gaps with social elements. We are born into (or from) some sort of familial unit, and then most often we seek to create our own, whether through offspring or friendships, driven by a societal link to others. We surround ourselves with people and things and identifications, offering opportunities to avoid feeling so alone.

The origins of our desire to break away from aloneness can be traced back to human evolution. Hominids who banded together to form tribes found that their chances of survival increased significantly over those who didn't mob up, and who later ceased to exist. This cooperation started as a means of survival, but perhaps it unlocked innate empathy and sympathy in our DNA. We see it in other animals that cooperate but also care for each other. Dolphins have been known to assist their females during pregnancy in a midwifery fashion; lions are often raised together in nurseries within a pride. The essential bond of cooperation and family is everywhere.

In my life, I have been very lonely at times. Perhaps it is just the nature of who I am. I didn't grow up alone—I had two parents and two sisters—but my condition was always one of solitude and yearning for companionship, a deeper connection perhaps than I felt to my own family. Much of this recognition about myself came in my adult years, and it is something with which I am still coming to terms. As a younger man, and as a boy before that, I had no clue what I needed. I would venture that few people do. I'm often reminded of a quote concerning maturity that has been attributed (although some say mistakenly) to Mark Twain: "When I was a boy of fourteen, my father was so ignorant I could hardly stand to have the old man around. But when I got to be twenty-one, I was astonished at how much he had learned in seven years." I am sure many of us have felt similarly about our own supposed journeys in maturity, and those of our parents, and yet I wish I had a better understanding of *me* at a younger age. In spite of my success (and I certainly don't mean to sound in any way ungrateful for all that life has brought me), I still wonder sometimes how my life would have turned out if I could have taken steps to mitigate that essential loneliness.

Even as our souls yearn for that bloodline bond to our relatives, the world does things to pull us apart. Instead of living and laboring on the family farm all of our short lives, now we have opportunities that compel us to branch out. They create physical and emotional distance from the core of this unit we have found so crucial to our survival as a species. You go off to university, which takes you away from home; you get a degree; and in your field, a job offer may present itself in another city, another state, another country even, and so off you go. Or you meet someone from a different place, and your desire to be with them, to begin starting your own family unit, compels you to follow them to their homeland. We gain something from fulfilling ourselves on professional and personal levels, but in doing so, we cannot help but rob ourselves of the close roots we had known.

I wish I'd had this awareness when I was younger. I lived at home until I graduated from McGill University in downtown Montreal at the age of twenty-one. I'm proud to say that all these years later, the student union center at McGill is known as the Shatner Building.

I never had a car during my early years, so I would take a twenty-minute streetcar from my home and walk to the campus. I did not attend quite as many classes as I should have, but I partook in all manner of extracurricular activities, largely centered around the arts department. After graduating, I did summer theater. From there, the manager hired me to go to Ottawa to do professional winter theater during the season. I got myself a car, moved all my belongings into it, and set off to seek my fortune. I networked with people based in Toronto who were organizing the Stratford Shakespeare Festival; they asked me to join them, and so, again seeking the next chapter of my journey, I went to Stratford, Ontario.

I remember feeling so isolated and lonely. Trying to make it on my own, I faced some of the most existential struggles of my life—literally. There were days when I would have to go without meals. I ate mostly at the five-and-dime; how much money I had in my pocket determined what I ate. Some days it would be coffee and toast for breakfast and then a small dinner at day's end, or a fruit salad for lunch, which would have to last me until the next day. I was struggling to survive, earning about $40 per week. From that I paid my rent and bills, put gas in my car, and tried to have enough left over for some semblance of a life, starting with food.

Years later, after *Star Trek* and my divorce from my first wife, I found myself in a similar existence, paying alimony and child support and living in my pickup truck with only my dog to comfort me. If you have ever been in such a position, you know that survival becomes your obsession. In some ways, that feeling never goes away.

Here's the thing: on some level, it doesn't matter how much wealth I acquire or how secure I feel at any given moment; in the next moment, I will feel that I am one step away from poverty. That's what living in a pickup truck can do to you. That's what being Jewish and growing up in the Great Depression and the time of the Holocaust can do to you. I wasn't told that life was fleeting; it was more something learned through osmosis. Being Jewish, I just had an understanding that at a moment's notice, you might need to go. When it came to financial security, you had to carry your skill, because one day, you might have to move quickly. The expression of that was evident in the favoring of certain careers over others: be in jewelry, so you can scoop it up and go; be in banking, so you can get out of town before they get you; be a doctor; be a lawyer—be something that allows you to carry your skills.

The idea of being Jewish and choosing *the performing arts* was not normal when I came of age. Even without that background, acting is a bit of a scofflaw profession. We are all beggars. It's the nature of the job. You're always begging:

"Can I have a job? I'd be perfect for that part! Look at my range!"

For a long time, mine was not a secure living by any stretch. My goal, for some arbitrary reason, was to see if I could get to $1,800 in my bank account. It would happen, especially during *Star Trek*, but with a wife, three kids, and a mortgage, it rarely lasted. After my first divorce, I fell on particularly tough times, and in those days, television shows didn't pay residuals when they were rerun. My life got desperate. I recovered, thank goodness, but that feeling in your gut of not knowing where your next meal was coming from, sadly, on some level, never really goes away.

As silly as it may sound, even though my family and I are taken care of financially, I still want to ensure I'm getting it right when it comes to money. I want to be paid what I think I'm worth; I want to save money on purchases where discounts are achievable. My survival instinct is still at play all these many decades later.

I wonder sometimes if my compulsion to do everything in my power to pursue my acting ambition was a point of pride, a subconscious desire to prove that my exodus from the comfortable family structure that had kept me fed and warm had to be *for something*. If we are programmed by nature to create and be part of these units for essential survival as well as comfort and some degree of happiness, then when we choose to disconnect from them in pursuit of something else, there must be a driving force that says we simply *must* achieve it. We risk so much just for the opportunity.

When confronted with the possibility of failure, as I attempted to navigate greener pastures in the entertainment industry, I would reassure myself that I could always go to Toronto and find enough local acting work to sustain me. I don't remember ever saying to myself, "Well, I can always go into business with my father and manufacture men's suits," or "I can always go home and sleep in my old bedroom." Those thoughts never occurred to me; in turn, it never occurred to me to give up. There wasn't anything *to* give up. I simply was not going to do anything other than perform.

What saddens me in hindsight is that when I went off to pursue these goals, I really did break some of those bonds without paying any respect to them. I didn't have the maturity to understand the deeper implications. I paid no extra attention to my family; I did not seek to compensate for my physical distance with more letters or phone calls. I wonder if my loved ones suffered for that. I have no doubt in looking back that I did.

In the last year, I have completed work on my latest album, *Bill*. (It's available on Spotify, Apple Music, Amazon Music—you'll be able to find it; go buy it or stream it or whatever you do with music these days!) I know the style of performance on my albums is not typical of singer-songwriters; it is more of a spoken-word poetry set to music. I've spent countless hours writing and refining the lyrics, and working with musicians to achieve the end result, and it is always incredibly meaningful to me. Each word, each phrase, each note, is chosen with purpose and deliberation.

I wrote a song on this album called, simply, "Loneliness." My vision was to express a sense of isolation, and originally, I had planned to do so in an orchestral fashion through what I believe to be the loneliest sounding string instrument: the cello. Something about the timbre of the cello reminds me of the wail of the wind or the cry of a loon. For me, it embodies that loneliness with which we are all born. I had written to Yo-Yo Ma to ask if he would play on the song, but his schedule did not permit it. From that, however—and I'll fill you in on the details in a later chapter—we found a completely different way of looking at and orchestrating that feeling of loneliness. Because we all feel it.

And yet.

There is family. There are friends. There are ways to mitigate the loneliness, to share in life experiences, and, as was expressed by actor Laurence Luckinbill as Sybok in *Star Trek V* (in one of its better moments, I believe), to "gain strength from the sharing."

I am fortunate: most of my own family is close by. Two of my three daughters live within a couple of miles of my house, while the other lives about fifty miles away—super easy to visit, barely an inconvenience.

My three daughters—Leslie, Lisabeth, and Melanie—and my wife, Elizabeth, are the absolute lights of my life. Each of my girls has such a distinctive personality that some people find it hard to believe they all had the same mother, but it's true. Their mother, Gloria, and I were divorced about twelve years into the marriage, after all three children had been born.

At this moment, most of my grandchildren also live within that same nearby circumference. I strive with objective knowledge to do what I didn't do all those years ago: to keep this wonderful unit thriving and to keep us all involved in each other's lives. During the worst days of the COVID-19 pandemic shutdown, when in-person gatherings were dangerous and prohibited, we turned to technology. Every Sunday, we met in a big Shatner Family Zoom. Often, we had as many as fifteen participants, each in their own window, with their own backdrop, talking, sharing jokes and stories, living that essential family life with a modern twist.

Some of our younger members were busy and

couldn't join each session, but I was filled with immense gratitude to see that my daughters have adopted the same mindset toward family that I now hold dear. All three are keenly family oriented and have kept their children and their father close. I feel truly blessed to be fully engaged in the continuation of these connections, which, as we know, are not always easy to achieve and maintain. The grandchildren are less intense about the need for our collective to thrive; I remember too well that I was the same way. It pains me sometimes that I am not the picture-perfect grandfather I want to be. Even at my age, I don't have all the answers. I cannot simply say to my grandchildren, "Yes, my dears. I have all the wisdom. Listen closely and I will tell you how it all goes." But I am trying. Every day, I am working to learn more, to be better, to fulfill the promise of my brief existence here on Earth.

Our children and grandchildren bring us so much. My favorite moments are when I am surprised. During the shutdown, certain parts of the world were opening up, while others were lagging. My eighteen-year-old granddaughter was in Italy as the nation began to emerge from the effects of the virus. She had gone there to learn Italian and to immerse herself in a different culture. It was her first foray away from home, and I was able to watch with fascination as she came into her own. In some ways, she went power mad with the autonomy she was presented with. She could make any decision she wanted, her possibilities limitless. I've tried to instill in her that the most rewarding aspects of this freedom are the choices she can make to continue to involve her family in her journey.

To my frustration, my Italian-adventuring granddaughter is often hard to reach, but recently she called me on FaceTime. She was in an Italian square somewhere in Rome, hanging out with three or four very good-looking young guys. There was my granddaughter, a being I have cradled from birth: a beautiful young woman, the center of attention of these boys. I instinctively jumped into playing grandfather.

"You'd better leave my granddaughter alone," I implored them, using a jocular (but really only half or quarter jocular) tone, "and get a haircut!" We all had a good laugh, and my granddaughter referred to me by some popular adolescent term. I don't remember if it was "You're the dope" (which I certainly am) or "You're the bomb," which sounds like a bad thing but is apparently a good thing. Either way, I took some comfort in knowing that I'd achieved a level of familial fame by being referred to in up-to-the-minute colloquial language.

My other granddaughters are a little younger, and we are close in different ways. One of them is very much an intellectual, and as I am always striving for knowledge in every possible way, I encourage those similar instincts in her. I send her articles and documentaries that resonate with me. I hope our shared interests tighten the bonds we have established, even as I recognize that there will be times when those bonds will stretch and fray. As she goes through those same experiences others do in that time of their lives, family will not seem as important.

As parents, we want to give our children better lives than we had. In my lifetime, as people moved out of the Great Depression, past the Second World War, and, in many cases, into prosperity the likes of which had never been seen, parenting began to change. Education went on longer, new industries emerged, and new activities for enrichment became available and affordable. For parents with means and time to support extracurricular activities, the possibilities were endless. They tried to enrich their children, encouraging them to try everything. Learn the violin. You don't like that? No problem, here's a trumpet. Hey, why don't you go outside and play baseball? You're not enjoying that? Give soccer a go. And then, for all that enrichment, research has shown that no matter which way or how hard their parents direct them, kids are going to figure out their interests on their own.

Certainly, you can expose your children to

different activities, but there seems to be a delicate line between ambition and encouragement. I knew so many kids in Montreal who were great skiers. They were pushed by their parents and took to it like ducks to water (Do ducks ski? Could they take to the ice?), but when they got older, they gave it up. It wasn't their ambition; it wasn't their interest. It was their parents who had hoped their kids would share their love of skiing and had encouraged them to become great at it. So, how can we ensure our children find fulfillment? We just don't know. When I was a child, I only wanted to act. Yes, I played football, and I tried other activities, but I had no illusions of making a vocation out of them. They were just activities I drifted in and out of. Like a stream, the water carried me along, but my end goal was always on the horizon. With clarity.

What I find charmingly ironic is that it was *through* my pursuit of acting that I was actually led to all manner of hobbies and interests that would not otherwise have crossed my mind. I have ridden motorcycles across the country, become an avid horseman, jumped out of airplanes, stood atop monumental peaks, traveled all over the world, renovated my house on camera, even peed out a kidney stone for charity and presented it on national television. These aren't the milestones one necessarily envisions as a child (at least not the kidney stone one), but they came to me in spite of my singular focus on one professional goal.

I don't know what to call that. Is it luck? Is it the universe looking after me, somehow? Encouraging me because I try to see and learn about my connection within it? That sounds a bit arrogant, I know. The truth is, I have no idea. As a result, when it comes to supporting my loved ones in their pursuits, I just try to be there for them—a steady hand at the ship, available to play father and grandfather, and to keep making mistakes as I attempt to get it right.

I also try to get it right in my marriage. I am fortunate that my daughters have been so understanding of their father's difficult love life. I was married to their mother, then divorced; they were partly raised by my second wife, and developed a strong bond with my third, Nerine, before her tragic passing. In 2000, I met Elizabeth Anderson Martin, a delightful soul with whom I shared so much in common—in both our passions and tragedies.

Elizabeth and I were both dealing with the heartbreaking loss of our spouses, her husband having died of cancer in 1997. Elizabeth was a brilliant horse trainer, which is how we met. We began a close friendship; she lived in Santa Barbara and I was in Los Angeles, so I would drive up, spend some time with her and her horses, have dinner, and then make my way back.

We were both still grieving from the loss of our loved ones, but it was a form of healing to talk to someone who was going through the same pain.

A short while later, I was invited by a *National Geographic* photographer to join an expedition to Antarctica. I called Elizabeth and invited her. "It'll be an adventure," I told her, assuring her that there would be separate staterooms and that I wouldn't try to redefine our relationship in the middle of an isolated continent from which escape would be impossible. Elizabeth debated the decision in a timeworn process she'd learned from her mother: she made a pros and cons list, and, unfortunately for me, the cons outweighed the pros.

What she didn't tell me at the time was how *badly* the cons outweighed the pros. "The cons were numerous," she later explained. "I didn't know you well; I owned a business and had a lot of responsibilities; I would be stuck on a boat in Antarctica. What if we didn't get along? What if it got awkward? What if something dangerous happened on the expedition? The only pros were that it might be an outrageous adventure and maybe I'd see some penguins."

Adventure and penguins. Nothing good about spending time with yours truly? I have to say, though, I admired Elizabeth's methods. Her pros and cons list hadn't let her down, and her process came from the heart. She just didn't think she should make the trip. I knew then that there was something truly special about this woman; just as this trip promised an adventure, the thought of getting to know her better seemed an even greater adventure. With much wailing and gnashing of teeth, I ultimately decided not to go. It was something akin to the line at the end of *Good Will Hunting*: "I had to see about a girl."

Some of you reading this may wonder why I continue to refer to Elizabeth as "my wife" when a cursory glance at Wikipedia or any number of websites will tell you that we are divorced. We are, in fact, divorced, but only on paper. Some may call it modern; others may call it strange; it was certainly a delicate concept to handle when we first went down this road, but we decided that to avoid any sort of conflicts whatsoever about my estate when I'm gone, we could separate our financial interests, leaving my three kids to inherit equally, while Elizabeth would be taken care of through the terms of the divorce. For us, it works, and I think that is all that really matters in the end.

Despite challenges over the years, my family unit is intact. I feel that I've done something right, hopefully for them as well as for myself; I have a clear vision of how I want my family to function, and of its importance to me. If you've ever seen a blade being forged, you'll know that it begins as a piece of steel. It is heated, beaten into shape, reheated, and left to cool slowly. The steel is heated and beaten again, and then again, quenched in liquid, sanded and sharpened, and then that perfect piece of steel can exist for a lifetime. That is the way I want my family to be. Even as I know perfection is an unattainable goal, I want us to be perfect in our construction. Perhaps striving for that is the best way of ensuring prosperity and contentment. I have long since passed the point where I have to work for myself, so everything I do, materially, is for my family, even as I continue to derive pleasure from the work itself.

I think about those video calls with my children and grandchildren. Modernity, in a strange contradiction, effectively tears us from our personal attachments, then comes right back to aid us through other applications. There I was, every week, talking to my family on Zoom while the pandemic kept us physically apart. Families all over the world can take advantage of technology to bridge the physical gap that exists between them as they move to different corners of the globe. When I was young, if you wanted to keep in touch with someone, you had to write them a letter; on rare occasions, if you had the money, you could manage a short phone call. Now? Communication has never been easier.

Sometimes, communication is so easy that we get ourselves in trouble. Jeffrey Toobin is CNN's chief legal analyst. When it comes to explaining constitutional law, he's got few peers and is well known for his sharp analyses. Unfortunately, in late 2020, Toobin became better known for an incident on a video call as part of his work for *The New Yorker*. He said he wasn't aware that his camera was still turned on when he inadvertently exposed himself to his colleagues. He was fired from *The New Yorker* and CNN, but later was welcomed back to the latter. We take video calls for granted now, but the exponential growth of technology has in some ways been driven by— wait for it—pornography. It sounds perhaps unlikely, but in an effort to fulfill our most basic needs for sexual satisfaction, we as a society have long enriched the coffers of companies that could deliver that content. I find this utterly fascinating. Here we have the synchronicity of a man being caught trying to gratify his most basic biological urges while using the very same innovation that likely fulfilled those urges.

For the record, I find it distasteful that we judge people by the worst moments in their lives. Certainly, the timing of Toobin's actions was unprofessional, but are we going to pretend that we do not have urges? My goodness, they are essential to our continued existence as a species. We are driven by a need to reproduce. Are we so prudish that we will publicly demand puritanism whereby sex can exist only in the context of procreation, while we flock in record numbers to view and consume pornography? I hope not. That seems to me an inherent denial of our basic humanity. It can only reinforce the loneliness that affects us all at various points in our lives.

In our early years, the essential aloneness into which we are all born is abated by the family unit. After that, how does one achieve that abatement? Our society says you get married. You have children. You surround yourself with more of your tribe, of your clan. You try to live a long life. When you die, your children continue the theme. Lather, rinse, repeat. Treated properly and nurtured along the way, that family unit can be the source of truly profound happiness; it is a tangible daily reminder of our connection to each other. A friend once remarked to me that if you could measure despair and joy on a scale of zero to ten, then without children in our lives, we would likely fluctuate between a two and an eight. Once children are factored in, that expands to the full zero-to-ten range. The highs are higher, the lows, lower. Being a father, I can say without question that this role has been the greatest, most fulfilling of my life. From that highest high to the lowest low, their joy is my joy, and their despair is mine as well.

I feel fortunate to be the father of girls at a time when the place of women in our society is inching closer to where it ought to be. I want my daughters and granddaughters to have the opportunity to fulfill themselves as human beings—something we menfolk have taken for granted since time immemorial. Progress is being made every day, even though, in my opinion, it is neither substantial nor swift enough. I dream that one day—it may unfortunately be a long time after I am gone—every one of you on this blue marble of ours will have the opportunity to achieve your maximum potential as a human being. It seems like such a simple proposition, and yet it has never been realized. *Star Trek* showed that in our imaginations, this idealism could one day become commonplace and accepted wisdom, to the point that it need not even have attention called to it. Gene Roddenberry once opined that "*Star Trek* was an attempt to say humanity will reach maturity and wisdom on the day that it begins not just to tolerate but take a special delight in differences in ideas and differences in life-forms." A more eloquent expression of the oneness of humanity, I have not found. We have the potential to find true unity of purpose and nature, but it requires that we all pay attention, especially those who sit atop the power structures.

While it is easier to maintain the status quo and not challenge our long-held beliefs, true progress and change require us to listen, to put aside our egos, to break deeply ingrained habits, and to see things from perspectives other than our own. It is not easy work. Certain elements are baked in and require significant effort to dislodge. I try to get it right, and I know I fail constantly. I recently caught myself using the term *authoress*. I used it as an identifier, certainly not with any derogatory intent, but I am reminded of the power of language, because language gives form to our thoughts, and to our attitudes. Those thoughts and attitudes are carried into our everyday lives, and they become the prevailing thoughts and attitudes of some of those around us as we seek to maintain our participation in societal units— friendships, family bonds, working relationships with colleagues. We can do better; we must do better. It is a challenge worthy of our highest efforts and attention.

I think often about "bonds" as we try to find connection. We now know that they exist on a far more elemental level than previously believed. Ecologist Suzanne Simard has spent her life unearthing fascinating facts about, for want of a better term, the secret lives of trees. We have long understood the vital role that trees play in our daily lives—taking in carbon dioxide, generating oxygen, and so forth. We have harnessed them for lumber, often in a manner that causes deforestation and damages the delicate balance of our planet. But through her tireless work, Simard has discovered, as documented in her absorbing book *Finding the Mother Tree*, the intricate networks through which trees communicate with each other. In their natural state, trees behave in very much the same way humans do. There is a central tree—the matriarch of the family, if you will—and around that central "mother tree," deep beneath the surface of the ground, are roots spreading out in myriad directions, connecting to all the other trees. Even when seeds are dropped in various places and scattered by the winds and displaced by birds and other animals, their eventual roots find their way back to the original connection: their mother tree. That mother tree, in essence, continues to try to take care of its offspring in a variety of ways, spreading nutrients and reinforcing the bonds through its ancient and time-strengthened roots, nurturing it to its potential. What is the tree's potential? To grow. To fulfill its purpose, to feel the warm, life-giving energy of the sun. A passage from Henrik Ibsen's *Ghosts* reminds me of this ever-upward thrust of trees and their desire to reach the potential imbued by their mother. At the end of the play, the character Oswald Alving begs his mother to euthanize him, so terrified is he to experience the effects of the disease syphilis, which is coursing through his body on the way to bringing him to a painful end. "Mother, give me the sun," Oswald entreats. She doesn't understand his request. "The sun. The sun," he repeats. To me, it feels like that most elemental need. The sun. Warmth. The need for love, and to be made to feel safe and comforted.

As a child, Suzanne Simard lived in British Columbia, Canada, where a tradition of clear-cutting the region's forests had been in place since the British first marched into the area and discovered there were woods. For decades, the loggers would simply cut down the trees and turn them into pulp and mulch. Over time, the people of the region came to understand, at least theoretically, that this would have an effect on the ecosystem. A government report cited the likelihood that the destruction of these swaths of trees could lead to permanent damage and erosion of the surrounding areas, which could create landslides and similar phenomena. A new policy was put in place: for every tree that was pulled down, another must be planted in its place. Hundreds of thousands were cut down, and hundreds of thousands planted to replace them. After graduating from university, Simard was hired to examine the plantings and to see how well the ecosystem was holding up.

Not well, she discovered. The replanted trees were struggling. Their roots were dying; Simard was determined to find out why. She experimented with different techniques, including digging up saplings and seedlings and examining their root structures. What she discovered was that, unlike the old trees that had been pulled down, the newly planted ones were not tightly connected to an existing root system. They didn't have their mother. Their family. It was taking longer for them to grow and they weren't connected to the rest of the trees the way they needed to be in order to thrive. If that isn't a metaphor for our own existence, I don't know what is. It just makes my spine tingle. Learning more about these connections we have to the fabric of trees, the fabric of Earth—I swear, it's why I wake up as early as I do and spring out of bed. That thirst for understanding powers me; in the vast universe of knowledge, I know nothing. I know a fraction of nothing. I need to learn more. In every discovery I make of the natural world, I find a connection to our own story—the story of our shared human condition.

We're told that time heals all wounds, that blood is thicker than water. Our bonds can break, but they can be healed. I have seen my own relationships bend and fracture, but also mend. A relationship can be saved by words and deeds, by working to create circumstances in which it can flourish. In the mirror image, when given the right conditions, the right nurturing, *nature* can regenerate. Bonds can heal. Fractures can mend. In the early twentieth century, it was governmental policy to exterminate many predators from Yellowstone National Park, which had been founded in 1872. By 1926, the Yellowstone wolf packs had all been wiped out. With the wolves removed from the landscape, the ecosystem began to change. Lacking a natural predator, the elk population skyrocketed. In the four decades that followed, almost seventy thousand elk were removed from Yellowstone (most, sadly, were killed, while some were introduced to other areas in which they'd previously been eliminated). In the late 1960s, the park reversed its policy and stopped killing and removing elk, leading their numbers to jump again. In harsh winters, many simply starved to death, and all the while, the ecosystem they depended on was gradually eroding, being stripped bare of all its natural sustenance by an elk population too big to spread the wealth effectively.

In the times before the predatory wolves were removed, the elk were often on the move, their numbers reduced by that predation. They didn't have time to browse the willows for long before having to move on. What this meant was that the willows had time to recover, particularly during winter months, and were available as a source of food for beavers. When the beavers were well fed, they built dams, which affected stream hydrology, providing a sustainable home for fish to thrive in, which in turn provided food for swooping birds and other creatures. The predatory wolves also effectively distributed food to other animals, leaving carcasses along the way to be picked at by birds, bears, and coyotes.

Without that delicate balance, those natural bonds started to break; the intricate network began to fray. In 1995, ecologists reintroduced the gray wolf to Yellowstone. Where before there was one beaver colony, today there are nine. The flow-on effect of the wolves' return has begun to rebalance the fragile Yellowstone ecosystem, to return it to its natural strength and continuity. It is a return to harmony and a physical reminder of the connection we share to the Earth and its inhabitants. As the ultimate apex predator, humankind has the most power to disrupt nature. I hope we can all learn a lesson in the futility of doing so and dedicate ourselves to repairing the damage we have wrought, generation after generation.

Mycologist Paul Stamets has been lauded for his pioneering work in the field of bioremediation—in essence, using mushrooms to help repair damage to the natural environment. These fungi produce enzymes that can break down pollutants and even, in some cases, *plastic.* Through his life's work in this fascinating field, Stamets has discovered yet another facet of how nature forges bonds and connections through what has been termed the "mycelial network." Fans of *Star Trek: Discovery* may remember the concept (and, of course, the tributary character Lieutenant Paul

Stamets, played brilliantly by Anthony Rapp), which was used in a theoretical fashion to allow interstellar travel in an instant, without the pesky long commute times associated with warp drive. Of course, the ability to travel through outer space along the mycelial network is pure fantasy (at present!), but the Paul Stamets of *our* century has shown how the mycelia of subterranean fungi connect plants and trees together, transporting nutrients, and effectively "talking" to those plants and trees, while providing a conduit for them to communicate with each other. He termed this connection "Earth's natural internet."

Plants and trees, fungi, and even some bacteria are said to communicate through low-level electrical impulses driven by their own chemical neurotransmitters. If that sounds familiar, it's because we have neurotransmitters in our brains. Our brains use neurons. They transmit. Simple, right? Except *what on earth does that mean?* Electricity generally is something we can harness, but there is still much to discover about how and why it exists in the first place. Similarly, our brains *exist* and we can harness them. They are built upon billions of electrical connections. It's easy to get lost in the technical jargon and theoretical nature of many of these discoveries and hypotheses, but what it all suggests to me is that we are part of this grand network, which we are only beginning to understand on a physical level. Our relationships, the bonds we forge and share with each other, are a microcosm for the inner workings of the universe itself.

Yet all of this somehow fails to capture the magnificence of that concept. It's so easy to say "we're all related." We try, failingly most times, to grasp at the implications of the concept, and yet it also seems somehow ingrained in all of us, if we can just look around and admire the grandeur of it.

I'm reminded of a trip I took to Ireland with my wife Elizabeth. We were in Dublin and were introduced to a reporter who wanted to show us some terrific spots around his country. So, we found ourselves in a small Irish village inn and met a gillie, a local fishing and hunting guide. I have hunted for sport in the past; it is one of my biggest regrets. I remain ashamed of myself for choosing to kill innocent creatures for no other reason than the challenge of proving my superiority. I try to adhere to a more plant-based diet these days, with occasional exceptions, and if I am to fish, it must only be for food. Never for sport.

The gillie asked if we had ever been fly-fishing. I had, many times: as a child with my father and later in Alaska with some of the world's premier fly fishermen. We agreed to go, having already decided that anything we caught would be our lunch. The gillie took us to a trout stream: "The best, most beautiful stream in the village," he said. He lent us fishing rods and took us through a little trail that ran alongside the stream. Every so often we would see a fly fisherman standing in the water, waders on, stalking the fish, waiting for his moment. There were maybe a dozen paths that led to spots where you could cast, and at each of them, a fly fisherman practiced his or her ritual.

Finally, we came to an empty area. We waded into the water with our equipment and began casting. After a couple of hours, we'd had no luck. No bites, no nibbles. Barely a ripple in the water. We couldn't catch so much as a cold out there. I asked if perhaps we should move on and seek better luck in another part of the stream. "Oh," the gillie replied, "I'm sorry if I've misled you. There are no fish in this stream."

Was this a joke? Were cameramen about to appear from behind the brush and expose me on an Irish trout-themed prank show?

"You see," the gillie elucidated, "I'm an alcoholic. All the people fishing here are alcoholics. It's a beautiful, peaceful place, and we come here to ease our minds by going into the fishing stream and casting about for fish that don't exist."

For them, it was a way to commune with nature, to distract themselves from their addictions, to try to find some peace. He explained that when the English had conquered Ireland during the

Elizabethan era, they had cut down all the big trees in this area to make masts for their sailing ships. Following the best wisdom of the time, they planted fast-growing trees to replace the ones they had removed, but these replacement trees had a different acid-alkaline balance. When the rains came, the imbalanced runoff flowed into the soil and into the streams, and the salmon that used to come up from the sea couldn't abide what these new trees were leaching into the stream. As a result of this disruption of the area's natural balance, they were diverted elsewhere.

The same story can be found throughout history. Cannery Row in Monterey, California; the Grand Banks in Newfoundland. Why do we do it? Why do we disrupt the very thing that holds all of our precious lives in balance? For progress, perhaps; out of ego, maybe. My only hope is that as we continue to learn from these experiences, we arrest similar propositions before they get out of hand. People often say we are destroying Earth, but what we're really destroying is ourselves. The elimination of species, the pollution of the atmosphere—all of this is ultimately destroying *us*. The planet will be just fine. It has survived through boom-and-bust cycles of humanity before. And believe me, the answer is not to go to other planets, because we'll probably just screw those up too if we're not careful.

But I digress.

The story of the alcoholic, fishless fly fisherman in Ireland hit all too close to the bone for me. It is true that given the right tools and conditions, nature's wounds can heal, as can the wounds in our own relationships and connections. But sometimes we just don't know what those tools and conditions are. In 1997, I married the most wonderful lady, a truly beautiful soul, Nerine Kidd. Nerine was addicted to alcohol and struggled constantly with this disease. I'd tried my best to help; I thought that my love for Nerine could "cure" her, but alcoholism is a powerful affliction. I had so much love to give, and yet all the love in the world could not conquer it. It is a disease that only those who have known it can really understand. I am not among them. I had only a dim understanding of it, at best.

I would research the best rehab centers, the best programs, and I would enroll Nerine. Nerine would try; she really would. She would go willingly, doing twenty-eight or thirty days without touching a drop of alcohol. I would pick her up and bring her home, and a few hours later, she would be drunk. It made me so miserable to watch this incredible, vibrant being destroy herself. She couldn't help it, and I just couldn't understand it.

In 2020, a popular question was making its way around the internet, asking whether or not each individual had an "inner monologue."

Apparently, most people said they did—they had a narrative voice running through their heads, asking questions, preparing their next statements, figuring things out. I had never experienced that. I speak and act extemporaneously—the words just arrive as I am saying them. Occasionally I will try to choose my words more judiciously, if I am trying to be particularly eloquent, or find a pretty phrase, or avoid putting my foot in my mouth. But I do not have an inner monologue; years ago, I thought the concept was a joke. Something used for that terrific gag in *Austin Powers* when Mike Myers's titular character speaks all his thoughts aloud after being unfrozen from "cryosleep."

At one point in Nerine's battle with addiction, she told me she no longer wanted to attend Alcoholics Anonymous meetings or try a new rehabilitation program. "I have a boardroom in my head," she told me. That was the phrase; I remember it clear as day: *a boardroom in my head.* "When I go to do something, the board has to decide. And they have different views. They don't agree. 'Shall I brush my teeth?' Yes, brush your teeth. *No, don't brush your teeth.* It never ends. Everything I do, the board has to deliberate. And they won't make a decision. I can't quiet the board." Then, resigned, she told me, "The only thing that quiets the board is a drink." I cannot fathom what that must have felt like. I had nothing to give but love and sympathy, but in the end, they were not enough to overcome alcohol's hold on Nerine.

As her drinking overpowered her, it became difficult for the two of us to function together. One morning, I left Nerine standing forlorn in the driveway. "I can't take you," I told her. "You've gotten drunk in front of the grandkids too many times." There was a look of such sadness on her face as I left. I went about my day and in the afternoon drove down to Orange County to spend some time with my eldest daughter, Leslie. After we went out for dinner, I made my way back to Leslie's place and phoned my house to check in on Nerine, but there was no answer. This wasn't unusual, but that didn't make it any easier when it happened. My daughters and I called family and friends, checking to see if Nerine had driven anywhere. There had been times in the past when she had been drunk and driven to one place or another; the police had usually found her passed out in her car and brought her home.

I drove back to LA to find my wife. Upon arriving home, the first thing I noticed was that the cars were all there. The dogs were in the kitchen. Nerine loved our dogs and they loved her; if she were in the house, they would have followed her. Why were they in the kitchen? Where could she have gone? Just then, the phone rang. It was Nerine's AA sponsor. I relayed the situation. "I can't find her."

"Have you looked in the pool?" the sponsor asked.

"No," I said, "but the gate is closed, and the dogs are up here in the house."

"Go look in the pool," she told me gravely.

I have told the story of my wife's passing before, but there are some details that are still so painful that I have mostly held off telling them. I went to the pool. It was opaque; there was a sliver of moonlight, but the pool was largely dark. I looked into the murky waters, barely able to make anything out. But in the deep end, I saw something. Even though I didn't want to believe it at first, my brain slowly began to tell me that it was a floating body. I held the cordless phone to my ear and told Nerine's sponsor: "Call 911."

I remember so vividly the terror of seeing her body. It was later determined that she had been in the water for a long time, and in thinking back, that made sense, because when I dived in and brought her back to dry land, she was *smaller.* Diminished. In the fraction of moonlight, her face had turned a light blue. This vibrant creature I had known was gone; her life force had evaporated.

Many months later, I sat alone in that pool, thinking of Nerine and the night she left my world. I got out of the water and sat by it. After about fifteen to twenty minutes, the pool had turned still. Motionless. I had the strongest flashback to the night of her death. When I had seen her body floating there, the water had been so still. So absolutely wrenching, even now.

It is in times of immense trauma that we rely on our shared bonds—when love *is* enough. I don't know what I would have done if I hadn't had my family around me. In a very natural, nurturing way, my three girls came to stay with me, and they surrounded me. I was never left alone. It was like a herd of elephants, who have been known to comfort one another when faced with loss, and to mourn their dead, surrounding the bereaved, sharing the pain and burden.

On *Star Trek* in the 1960s, we had a cinematographer by the name of Gerald "Jerry" Finnerman. He was one of the youngest working cinematographers in television, an extraordinarily talented artist. He later moved from *Star Trek* to *Mission: Impossible*. In 1969, Jerry was on a small plane with members of a television crew on their way to a location scout in Colorado. The plane crashed; Jerry was the sole survivor. He endured a long and difficult rehabilitation, but continued his incredible work, later being inducted into the Producers Guild Hall of Fame. He passed away at the age of seventy-nine in 2011. He was a wonderful man and we had a close working relationship.

I remember one day on the *Star Trek* set, I received a fateful phone call: my father had died in Miami, where my parents had moved some years before. The earliest flight I could get out of Los Angeles was a few hours away. I didn't want to simply go to the airport and sit alone with my grief. I decided to stay, to try to distract myself with work, and yet the words could not escape my mouth. I couldn't be Captain Kirk. I could barely hang on to being Bill Shatner. As I stood there, unable to function, Leonard Nimoy and Jerry came over to me, and like two elephants, they stood shoulder to shoulder, cocooning me between them, holding me up. It was a beautiful, touching moment that I still think of, and it was a similar experience when my girls came to take care of me after I lost Nerine. I am fortunate that in my life I have lived through some of the greatest triumphs one can imagine. And yet, along with the best moments, I have encountered some of the absolute worst. I think about that fateful night a lot. What could be worse than finding your spouse's body? Only losing a child, I would presume, but that is a thought I will dismiss as fast as I have raised it.

Nerine's passing was a reminder to me that despite our best efforts, there are wounds to our family bonds that cannot be healed. While family can be the glue that holds us together and gives us respite from our innate loneliness, sometimes family can be alienating, whether through your actions or theirs. If your family disowns you, or you them, you are destroying those essential bonds. They are hard—not impossible, but hard—to rebuild.

The family unit long ago became a very useful tool for literal survival, and still operates that way in the years when children rely on their parents to keep them alive. For the most part, the instinct of human families is not to rear their children to be able to survive and then move on; family members expect to remain part of each other's lives for the long haul. We continue to rely on the nurturing from the links we have created for stability, understanding, cooperation, and mental health. We branch out, broadening those connections through marriage, which, in effect, brings a stranger into the expanding family unit. The stranger may have been brought up in a different way, with different values, different conceptions of what is and is not important. Sometimes this new member prevails upon their spouse, and it can lead to a break in the family connection. A parent may see their child as "taken away" by their spouse because they are more enamored of the tether to the spouse than to the rest of their family.

In many cases, we make a new family, consisting of friendships. A true friend is very hard to come by; at times there will be an imbalance, and there is a temptation, out of necessity or greed, for one person to exploit that imbalance for their own gain. It might be one friend only ever talking about themselves, or asking for a few too many unreciprocated rides to the airport (and as anyone in Los Angeles knows, a ride to LAX is one of the truest expressions of love and friendship you can find!). A friend might borrow a sum of money, say $1,000, to help them through a difficult time. Now that friendship has a price. If that money doesn't come back, for the lender friend, that is the price of the friendship. But the borrower friend may have a different perspective. "Look how easily he loaned me this $1,000. I really needed it; he didn't need it, so there's probably no need for me to pay it back immediately, or at all." There the cracks emerge.

Friendships are probably different from family in this regard. Parents are often advised not to guarantee their children's loans, no matter how much they might want to help them. Yet even if they do, the familial bond is often strong enough that in spite of whatever misgivings follow if the loan is never repaid, the parents do not stop being parents, and despite their profound disappointment and maybe even loss of trust, they very likely do not stop loving their children. Mothers in particular have a reputation for forgiving almost everything because they gave birth to you. That beguiling moment when a baby first looks at its mother is built in; that original bond is almost impossible to break.

I sometimes wonder if Timothy McVeigh's mother still loved him even after he murdered 168 people and wounded hundreds of others when he bombed the Alfred P. Murrah Building in Oklahoma City in 1995. As they took McVeigh to his execution, I wondered if he thought about his mother. Did he call for her? Or even in the face of death, did he remain steadfast in his sociopathy and the evil deeds he had chosen, completely detached from the humanity he had discarded so recklessly? As a parent, can you give up on an evil child? Can you break that bond by choice, even though it is so ingrained, because the pain of continuing it is just too much to bear?

For many, religion offers answers. I do not consider myself religious. At times, I wish I had the certitude of those who are, because believing with all your being that you have the answers, that you know all the wonderful things that will happen to you when you finish your corporeal existence here on Earth, sounds very comforting. I think of myself as Jewish but in a more cultural, traditional, perhaps ethnic sense. I'm Jew-ish. (I didn't invent that joke, of course, but I do love it.) To this day, scholars in the Jewish community continue to debate whether Judaism is actually a religion. "It's a religion." "It's a way of life." "It's a community." "It's an ethnicity." "It's a shared history." "It's a love of bagels." The debate goes on.

Even Israel, the ancient and now modern Jewish homeland, is home to both a religious and a secular community; its government has been headed by three *atheists* who nonetheless considered themselves Jewish. Golda Meir was once asked, "Do you believe in God?" and she replied, "I believe in the Jewish people, and the Jewish people believe in God." But do we? What are we Jews to make of this identification of ours? I don't know. But I won't say no to a nice bagel with a schmear.

I tend to fall back on a sense of being spiritual. I believe we're all connected to the universe in some way, and we're learning more about those connections every day, but we don't have all the answers by any means. I believe in the mystery: the awesome question of why we're here and how we're connected. Perhaps we are here to observe the glory of the universe. When I learned about the connection between the trees and the mycelia—the mother tree connecting its roots and nutrients to the other trees, nurturing them to their potential—and I saw the parallels in our own bonds as human beings in our groups and our families, I could not help but weep. From happiness. From the richness of being alive to ask these questions and explore these fundamental mysteries.

It is not a new idea to posit that we are all interconnected. For centuries, the Native American

Lakota tribe has believed in the circular nature of existence and expressed this in one of their mantras, *Mitakuye Oyasin*: "We are all related." What thrills me is how we continue to see the proof of this idea coming to fruition through scientific method. When we learn these things, it provides us with a chance to get back to those connections. To nature, to our friends, to family. Whenever those opportunities present themselves, I beg of you, *seize them*. Carpe those diems. You'll miss them when they're gone.

— CHAPTER 2 —

LISTEN TO THE ANIMALS

I have a passion for animals. My love of horses is well known; what is perhaps less known is that I got my first horse by accident.

As I started to enjoy some success in the entertainment industry, my second wife, Marcy, and I decided that it might be nice to own a beach home—somewhere we could head to with the kids to spend a vacation. We started driving up the Pacific Coast Highway in Southern California, looking for our future second home. But all these places were expensive—perhaps not by today's standards, but very expensive for the early eighties! We drove farther and farther north, and every time we saw something available, the price was so far beyond our means it felt like the universe was playing a cruel joke on us.

And yet, as I have mused, somehow, the universe has always looked out for me. Think of it as fate, think of it as karma, or think of it as Mr. Spock once did when he said, "There are always possibilities." To explain how this particular possibility arose, how I was seemingly in the right place at the right time to accept this gift from the universe, I must take you back a couple of years to before Marcy and I found ourselves traveling up the highway in search of a nonexistent beach house in our modest price range.

I had received a phone call from a young actor, David Fox-Brenton; he had come from the Stratford Shakespeare Festival in Ontario, where I had been a member of the company, and he wanted to start a Shakespeare Festival in California. David told me, "There's a town in California called Stratford, right in the center of the state, and I think it would be the perfect place for a festival. Will you help me?" As is my custom, I said yes. A few weeks later, he reported to me from Stratford, "It's two gasoline stations and very little else, but there's a beautiful, lush city thirty miles away in the heart of the San Joaquin Valley called Visalia. Let's do it there!"

I traveled up to Visalia and helped David raise money to put on the Stratford Festival. Visalia is one of the most fertile, most beautiful farm areas in the world. When I was there, working to find funding for the festival, I noted a common refrain from the locals that this here was God's country, and that I should really think about buying property up here. *Yeah, yeah,* I thought. I didn't want a farm; I wanted to live by the ocean.

So fast-forward, it's now years later and we're looking for a home, without success. I said to Marcy, "You know, we're never going to find a beachside home. Why don't we try somewhere near Visalia?" Our next stop was a restaurant about fifty miles north of Visalia, across the street from a real estate office. As it was Sunday, the office was closed. Nearby, however, folks were just coming back from the local church. They were standing around, saying goodbye, wishing each other well, and some were getting ready to attend their post-church luncheons. I ran over and asked if anyone knew who worked at the real estate office. A very nice lady raised her hand and said it was her office.

"I know you're closed," I said, my tone imploring, "but I'm a real live customer. I'm in the market for a home and some land." I don't know if it was the impassioned performance I'd like to think only a William Shatner could give, or if she needed the commission, or if it was simply because she was a kindhearted person, but this lady gave up her Sunday celebration and took us out to look at properties. We followed her about twenty miles outside of this small town, where she showed me a property that met the qualifications I was looking for: it was private, and it was on a river, and we could afford it. We bought it.

That property has become part of our family, our gathering place. It's on a wild river with no neighbors for miles, and it's where I keep most of my horses. It's part of the Shatner family, and all because I happened to spend some time raising money for a Shakespeare festival (which, sadly, lasted only a few years and then closed). But my connection with that area endured and it became part of my life. Somehow, the universe had put me in the right place at the right time, and all I had to do was say yes to begin this great adventure.

Okay, so I've got the land. How did I get the horse, you ask? I'm getting there, I'm getting there.

There was a small tract house on the land, which I rented to a local fellow I thought would take good care of the property, which he did. Later, we put a fence around the whole area, and the renter suggested, "Why don't you run a horse?"

"Great," I said, "I'll get a horse."

Now, how does one *get* a horse? At auction, apparently.

By this time, on my trips back and forth, I had met a very rich hotelier, who had a son named Phillip. Phillip was eleven or twelve years old and was something of a savant with horses: he could communicate with them on an entirely different level from the rest of us. This boy couldn't pick up on regular social cues that you and I might take for granted, but there was a bond he shared with horses; somehow he knew what they wanted and how to take care of them. When we went to a local auction several miles away, Phillip was there, examining the horses, talking with the locals, and having a great time.

We settled in, and at one point, a striking quarter horse came up for auction. Phillip caught sight of me in the audience and waved. "Mr. Shatner, you should buy this horse." I smiled politely. This *was* my first rodeo; I didn't want to get into things too hastily. I wanted to relax, see what it was all about, make an informed decision—

"Mr. Shatner! Mr. Shatner! You should buy this horse!" Phillip exclaimed. Trying to be polite, I waved him off—

"Going once . . . going twice . . . sold!"

I smiled and clapped at the auctioneer's gavel. Someone had just bought this lovely animal and was presumably going to enjoy a wonderful time bringing it into their family.

And that someone was me!

You see, when I had waved politely to Phillip to indicate that I wasn't going to jump into the bidding, I was inadvertently raising my hand, which the auctioneer took as a bid. That *sold!* was directed at me, the guy with the surprised, goofy look on his face. It was embarrassing, a TV trope that has been done to death—the schmuck who accidentally wins an auction. And *I* was that schmuck. I had just won a horse I hadn't actually bid on!

I sat there for what seemed like an eternity, struggling with the thought of what to do next, torn between the embarrassment of saying, "Sorry, I was actually just waving to my friend's kid," and buying this horse and bringing it home. I chose the latter.

That horse was wonderful. He was the first of many more to come. This happy accident led to a part of my life that has brought me so much joy I can scarcely believe it; it sometimes makes me cry just to think about it. Today, at ninety-one, I am a better rider than I've ever been. Perhaps it's because I know that I have well and truly entered the final chapter of my life, but I am more focused when I'm riding than ever before. I am getting better each day, reaching my apex.

It has been said that one of the secrets to staying alive as you get on in years is keeping busy. I am one busy dude, so I confirm this is the case. I work every day, and even though I'm an early riser, unless I have specific commitments, my actual workday usually begins after lunch. In the morning, after my regular ablutions, I head out to my horse trainer's farm to work with one of several horses. If I'm lucky, I can go out there six days a week, and I try to do that anytime I'm not traveling. I'll work with a horse for two or three hours and only then come back to get ready for the rest of my day.

But to me, this is much more than keeping

busy. It is not a function of scheduling. I have to commune with my animals. I have to learn from them, just as I hunger to learn in every aspect of my life. My work schedule often takes me away from my home, but I always endeavor to hurry back as soon as I'm able. If I am not sitting on a horse at least once or twice a week, it feels detrimental to my heart. These animals are capable of communicating with pure love, just as that tiger shark was in those moments when I stroked its belly and caressed it. There is something unifying in that love, that energy. It gives me life and keeps me feeling younger than I have any right to feel.

Horses are incredible creatures. Our history is filled with stories of humankind's connection to these stately beings and their capacity for love and kinship. There was a horse during the Korean War who traversed a mountaintop ridge over fifty times to drop off munitions and collect wounded soldiers to transport them to safety on her return journey. In the midst of exploding shells, in the deadliest throes of battle, this horse continued in this pattern of going up and down the mountain. She wasn't led or ridden; she just *did this* for her people. The horse was later made a sergeant in the Marine Corps—they named her "Sergeant Reckless." It is a well-known story of the war, and so sad that it has to be associated with such a bloody and violent time, but I do believe it speaks to the innocence and innate compassion of these creatures. They want to help us; they want to experience a connection with us. The eminent Sergeant Reckless, a true American hero, has been the subject of numerous books, both for adults and children of all ages.

Likewise, there is a beautiful story of a horse trained to compete in equestrian reining competitions who, in his later life, was renamed "Blind Justice" because he had gradually lost his sight. And yet he was known for running into the arena, his owner on his back, and sliding to a complete stop at a certain point. It was a move he'd learned in his youth from his owner; they had done it so many thousands of times that even as he lost his sight, the horse continued to execute this maneuver flawlessly and without even an iota of lost confidence in his ability to slide to that stop in exactly the right place. So completely had he given himself to his rider, it seemed, that he knew that no harm could befall him while his rider had the reins.

These stories are plentiful. These types of interactions occur on a daily basis if we are lucky enough to open our eyes to the possibilities, to witness and receive that love.

Through my work with horses, I have seen that love up close. I have seen it transferred to others, and it is a miracle to behold. Many, many years ago, I had been at a horse show that raised funds to benefit a hospital in downtown Los Angeles that employed therapy horses in treatment. That year, the lady directing the event said that it had become too difficult and expensive to continue. In my usual impulsive way, I volunteered to take it over, and the Hollywood Charity Horse Show has been running and raising funds for horse therapy ever since. Through this charity work, I have seen things I had not believed were possible. Perhaps the most profound was when a six-year-old girl who had been born without arms and with only one leg rode one of our horses. The therapy team—it takes at least three people in a case like this, due to the physical labor involved—led the horse with this child on top of it. She gripped the reins with the toes of the one foot she had, and the most unbelievable smile broke out across her face. For me, it was another one of those *wow* moments; for her, it must have felt like she could fly.

I've been asked why horses can have such a profound effect as therapy animals. Although other animals, particularly dogs, are used for therapy purposes, there is something about the majesty of horses that seems to invite patients to come out of their shells. If one has a physical, mental, or developmental disability, or is otherwise unable to experience events the same way those without disabilities do, there is something about the regal bearing of a horse that can open up the mind and the heart. It is a chance to experience basic connections and interactions that may have otherwise been elusive, and it occurs on such a primary level. You can watch one of these horses and imagine it sweeping across prairies; they are such stunning animals that many patients cannot help but become enthralled by their beauty. Once they are astride and seemingly in control of them, they feel an amazing power. For someone who may experience challenges in their daily life, to experience oneness with such a large, dynamic creature can make them feel ten feet tall.

The experience goes beyond riding. In therapy sessions, patients are given the opportunity to interact with horses in every aspect of their lives. They feed them, bathe them, and scrub them, and as you can imagine, an animal responds to that love. It gives love back. It nuzzles, it whinnies in appreciation, and the patient receives that love, a love that reminds them that there is more to life than any limitations they've previously held on to. The transference of that energy is so powerful to behold: one giving love and being loved in return.

In horse therapy, we have begun to do what is called "therapeutic vaulting," which is essentially having a patient, usually a child, perform simple gymnastics while the horse trots lightly around a paddock. There are adults in front and on the sides for support, but these children are doing something they've likely never dreamed of in their wildest imaginations. I have seen it on their faces, that look that perhaps things they didn't think could be possible might just be. I have seen kids who couldn't walk take a few steps; others who wouldn't talk speak a few words. It is the most miraculous sight to behold, and I promise you, you do not need to have children to look on in awe and wonder. The symbiotic effect of two of Earth's beings meeting and gaining love from each other is extraordinary.

I have found that bearing witness to these events activates a bond deep within me. I feel, in just a small part, that I have been a guardian figure to both the horses and those incredible, beautiful people who sit atop them. It renews my spirit and reinforces my feeling that we really are all connected to each other in some indescribable way. Human beings, animals, the earth on which we tread, the air we breathe: we were all made for each other, if we could only grasp and remember that notion.

The application of horse therapy has had profound effects not only on children with disabilities, but on returning veterans traumatized by the terrible experiences only war and combat can bring. We used to call it "shell shock," but it is now known as post-traumatic stress disorder (PTSD). These wounds are not the physical kind, but they are often the ones that are most difficult to heal; in many ways, they simply never do. Certainly, there are degrees: a soldier who is surrounded by love and family likely has a better shot at getting through the rest of their days than one who goes without that love. Sometimes, the best therapy is with animals. There is something they know that we haven't quite figured out. I believe it is that they know how to love unconditionally.

In therapy, these veterans—often people without limbs, or with profound PTSD, who find it difficult to interact with people, or even leave their homes—get on a horse, and once they do, they encounter an experience completely different from the rest of their lives. Sitting astride, they find themselves moving effortlessly. They're higher up, they're moving; it's almost as if they are on a different plane. A veteran who can't walk feels as if they can glide. The look on their faces is one of unmistakable joy, of unbridled enthusiasm and happiness. These men and women, who have returned from horrendous conditions in which their everyday tasks were to stay alive and to be prepared to kill, can suddenly relax in a way they had never imagined. It doesn't last forever, but for those moments, it is pure love; it is everything.

I have learned, tragically, that love alone cannot bring someone back from such trauma, but the kind of pure love that these animals express can go a long way toward some measure of healing. I wrote earlier of the tragedy that robbed me of my wife Nerine, and how I believed that my love could save her and found out that it could not. In the wake of her death, I established what became the Nerine Shatner Friendly House, one of two Friendly House residential programs for women recovering from substance and alcohol abuse. The houses are a safe space for many women, all dealing with their own struggles and looking for a place to feel supported. Since 2018, we have connected many addicted women with horse therapy through our Saddles for Serenity program, a modality based on the Twelve Steps of Alcoholics Anonymous and the use of horses for healing, self-awareness, empowerment, and transformation for sobriety and other addictions. I feel privileged to have heard from many of the women in the programs, who have written to me and spoken about the miracles that have occurred when they work through their afflictions through horse therapy.

To think that what became a lifelong passion began with a simple misunderstanding and a hint of embarrassment is so striking to me. I bought this horse by accident all those years ago, and because of that, I have been blessed so many times over with the love of these animals, and the gift of witnessing that love make its way to so many others. How many other quirks of fate have handed us a lifetime of opportunity, and what is the cost of ignoring these flickers of chance when they appear?

It is one of life's beautiful synchronicities that love can go both ways. We have all seen stories of abused, abandoned animals, who seem shattered by circumstance and their poor treatment, only to turn into the most affectionate of creatures when given a chance to express their love. I know a young couple with a similar passion for animals who have rescued and re-homed many cats and dogs.

I was struck by one of their rescue stories, in which the woman, Elizabeth, brought home a little Chihuahua/Jack Russell mix. She was eighteen months old and had lived on the street for twelve months and in the pound for six months, alone in a tiny concrete block covered in newspaper. The dog, whom they later named Lola, was understandably terrified and confused. She had been spayed by the shelter while pregnant (which must have been especially traumatic), and because animals tend to react poorly when folks stick their hands into their cages, Lola had bitten a would-be adopter who had come to consider her. As a result, the shelter deemed that Lola was "aggressive," and she was scheduled to be put to sleep. Elizabeth had been tracking her through the shelter's website, and when Lola's last day came, and there was still no one to adopt her, Elizabeth raced to the shelter. She didn't have a plan for how to re-home this dog; she just knew she could not allow her to be killed.

Dog shelters are heartrending places. The dogs are frightened, and the workers, who deal with so much death and sadness, can sometimes become desensitized and jaded. So it was with Lola: even though Elizabeth had arrived and offered to adopt the dog, the shelter worker told her that the paperwork had already been filed, and thus they could not release the dog, and instead had to put her down as scheduled. Elizabeth raised holy hell; eventually common sense prevailed, and they released the dog to her.

Lola was so terrified that she would lash out at anyone who got near her. To take her home, Elizabeth had to wrap her up in a blanket. For the first four days, it was virtually impossible to get anywhere near Lola for fear of losing a finger. She would not eat and would drink only enough water to get her through the day. And she *stank,* as you can well imagine. Finally, Elizabeth decided that enough was enough. "To hell with this," she said to the little dog. "You're getting a bath."

Elizabeth filled the tub, again wrapped up Lola (who kicked and screamed the whole way to the bathroom), and got into the warm water with the dog. And then something happened.

Something incredible. Once Lola was in the water, everything changed. For this animal, whose faith in human beings had been destroyed, who was on her way to her death, the warmth of that water must have felt like the amniotic fluid of the womb. This puppy was suddenly bathed in warmth, being held, being made to feel safe. She looked up at Elizabeth almost as if to say, "Oh . . . oh, I'm yours." From that moment on, she just melted. She realized she was home. She had found her person. She had found love.

Animals can teach you everything about devotion. In some ways, you don't find them; somehow, they find you. And then they decide that you are linked by an unmistakable, pure love. Dogs and horses and all kinds of animals bury themselves into our hearts, and sometimes our relationships with them are the most meaningful of all. Even the stories of other people's relationships with their animals can move us to tears. How many hundreds of thousands, maybe millions, have been touched by the statue of the dog Hachikō, who waited every day for nine years for his deceased owner at the train station in Shibuya, Tokyo? It's a story none of us experienced firsthand, and yet it is enough to bring tears to our eyes because we know that love. It's almost too much to bear. I have found it difficult to watch the numerous films in which the story of Hachikō has been memorialized.

I once appeared with my surviving *Star Trek* cast members on an episode of *Futurama*, a show as truly heartwarming as it was funny and clever. In the same season as our appearance, *Futurama* aired an episode called "Jurassic Bark," in which the character Fry (voiced so perfectly by Billy West), who in the show had been cryogenically frozen in the twentieth century and unfrozen in the thirty-first, finds a fossil of his old dog ("Seymour Asses") and seeks to have him cloned. At the end of the episode, after learning that Seymour, who was three years old when Fry was frozen, eventually lived to fifteen, Fry assumes that his dog ultimately found a new owner and forgot about him. Yet, in a clear homage to the story of Hachikō, the episode ends with a montage of Seymour spending the next twelve years waiting for his owner to come back; tragically, he never did. *Futurama* is, on its surface, a comedy, but in moments like that, it is among the finest human stories ever presented. Truthfully, it is so emotional that it is almost impossible to revisit.

When it comes to our relationships with animals, we are allowed to enjoy the euphoria of the bonds we form with them, but at the cost of enduring the heartache of agonizing loss. Indeed, for many children, their first experience with the concept of death comes when a pet dies. This may be an apocryphal story, but it's always felt true to me. Upon losing a beloved dog to cancer, a grieving family wondered aloud why dogs live only a fraction of a human life span. A six-year-old child is said to have remarked, "People are born so that they can learn how to live a good life—like loving everybody all the time and being nice. Dogs already know how to do that, so they don't have to stay for as long as we do."

I wish it had been so easy when that moment first arrived in my childhood.

I was a very lonely child who did not have a quintessentially loving relationship with my parents. We weren't estranged by any means, but for whatever reason, I did not feel the love I needed when I was growing up. Perhaps seeking to fill that void, I had always wanted a dog, but my parents said no. "Dogs bring in dirt," my mother would tell me. "We don't want more dirt in this house." My father, who worked very hard to provide for the five of us, doubtless thought of a dog as yet another mouth to feed, another entity to provide for. To someone whose sole focus was working and saving to make sure his family was safe, a dog, understandably, had no purpose.

Yet somehow, even though we didn't get a dog, a dog found *me*. It was a homeless mutt who hung around our neighborhood in Montreal, often playing in the yard behind ours, which was accessible from the street. I would walk ten blocks home from school and hop the fence to play with "my dog." She didn't live with us and my parents didn't have to pay for her (so they were perfectly okay with the arrangement), but she was my dog. I'd put out water for her, play fetch, wrestle with her, and often save food from my school lunch just to make sure she had some sustenance. All I wanted to do each day was come home from school to play with that beloved dog.

One day, I came home and hopped the fence, but she was nowhere to be found. I went back to our house, where my mother was waiting for me. I'll never forget the look on her face. She had to tell her child, the way all parents do eventually, that nothing lasts forever. She said simply, sadly, "Your dog is in the street." I didn't quite understand the meaning behind her words, except perhaps instinctively, but I ran out to the street so I could go see my dog. And there she was, lying on the road, dead, having been hit by a car and left there.

I sat down and held her. I hadn't known death; I hadn't ever been confronted with it. Finally, I picked her up and carried her toward my house. We lived in a fourplex, and underneath the balcony of one of the upper houses was some latticework. I crept under the balcony and sat with my dog, the late afternoon sun streaming through the latticework in a dappled pattern. It illuminated her in an angelic way as I held her, rocked her, and sang to her. I hadn't known death, and I really hadn't known life. My parents were very protective and sheltering, and I wasn't prepared for the emotion of experiencing this kind of permanent loss. This moment came at me so suddenly that it was overwhelming. To this day, I am affected by the memory of losing that dog. It was almost eighty years ago, and yet I had to stop in the middle of writing this story, so overcome by the recollection, and weeping as I thought of it.

Yet in the midst of this sadness, my resolve to once again feel the unconditional love of a companion animal was stronger than ever. Later, when I was married and had the means, I finally set out to bring a dog into my life. In February 1953, I had seen a *Time* magazine article about the Westminster Dog Show, in which a Doberman pinscher named Storm from the Rancho Dobe kennel in California had swept the awards. Some years later, as an actor living in Los Angeles, I spent a lot of my time driving. From one side of town to another. Auditions, studios, from the Valley to downtown for a show—it's a lot of time behind the wheel. (And it's immeasurably worse for young actors now, given how bad traffic has become in the last forty years.) In those days, the Ventura Freeway went to a certain point at the end of the San Fernando Valley and stopped. Right there at the end of the freeway, I saw a sign that read RANCHO DOBE. What were the odds? I thought, *Is this a sign?* Well, yes, of course it was a sign—it was clear as day right off the freeway.

I drove in and met the owner (whose name was Elizabeth, which makes me feel like the name Elizabeth and animals just go together from birth). I asked if she had any dogs. She said, "Well, no, this is a big kennel where we breed show dogs, and all the dogs are spoken for. But I do have a cull—one of the puppies who won't be a show puppy. I'll give him to you."

I took this puppy home and named him Morgan. Morgan lived with me for fifteen years. He was such a friendly dog, and always very aware of his surroundings. He'd leave the house, go out into our Hollywood Hills neighborhood and play with the kids, then always return back home for supper. Morgan was an incredible, almost-human animal. I kept in touch with Elizabeth and told her I had an interest in one day showing Dobermans in competitions. She came to visit and saw Morgan interacting with the locals. "I have to tell you," she said, "Morgan is the best ad for a Doberman I have ever seen."

I learned later that Morgan had been spending time with a young boy who was having difficulty at school and at home. It was like he knew what the boy needed, and he was there to provide it. It reminded me so much of the dog who came into my life when I was also a young child, in desperate need of the love that only an animal can understand and provide.

Dogs have an incredible empathy. You could argue that it's been bred into them because of domestication, but studies have shown that it goes well beyond that. There are dogs that can sniff cancer; they can empathize with things you don't even know are happening. Several years ago, my wife Elizabeth and I both underwent separate cancer scares, and we traveled to Philadelphia to spend time with cancer-sniffing dogs at the University of Pennsylvania's Penn Vet Working Dog Center. The dogs "told" us what was only discovered later after more tests—that neither of us had cancer, and instead had both been the victim of false positive readings. Imagine that: a dog knowing better than modern medical machinery. Yet this is not an uncommon occurrence. Dogs have been known to smell high blood pressure and other sorts of diseases. Their senses of smell are hundreds of times better attuned than ours, and evidently some of these ailments give off certain odors. It's been said that when you're cooking pasta sauce, a human can smell the tomatoes, but a dog can smell each individual ingredient. During the first year of the COVID-19 pandemic, the Finnish government experimented with COVID-sniffing dogs at the airport. A French study in 2021 reported that trained sniffer dogs scored 97 percent accuracy in sniffing out COVID in armpit sweat. A tough gig, but a noble one.

Even for those who have experienced the death of animals, there is still only so much that can prepare you for when you must go through that pain again. I have been there for my animals at the beginning of their lives, and I consider it my sacred duty to be there in their deaths. Sometimes a dog becomes so ill, and its quality of life marred by such constant pain, that we are led to the difficult but humane decision to put them to sleep. I believe with every fiber of my being that you must be there for the end. If possible, seek out a vet who will come to your home to administer the end-of-life medication. It is almost too painful to say, but there are stories of dogs that are brought to the vet to be put down, and in their final moments, they cast their eyes about, looking for their owners, confused, frightened, and needing reassurance. I beg of you, if you take one thing from this book, take away that you cannot allow that to happen.

Even at the end of their lives, dogs are selfless. They want to be there with and for you at the end. I had a Doberman named Starbucks, who lived to the age of fifteen. He almost died while I was out of town, but somehow, like an old parent waiting for their child to come to their bedside before drawing their last breath, Starbucks held on while I raced home from the airport. I sat on the floor with him and Elizabeth, and the two of us held him and crooned as he went in and out of consciousness. We petted him, his eyes opened and then closed, and as he passed on, we held his paw and looked into his eyes. He didn't need to cast about in fear; he had us, and we had him. He died peacefully in our arms. Ours were the last eyes he ever saw, our bodies the last he ever touched. I believe he took his final breath feeling at home, secure, loved. As he had been in life. Elizabeth and I wrapped Starbucks in a sheet and buried him near a tree in our backyard, not far from where we'd buried another dog who'd lived for almost the same number of years.

Today I have two young dogs, Espresso and Macchiato (you've likely picked up on a theme), and they bring me untold joy every day. Our dogs are our companions, and like that young boy once said, they already know how to love with all their hearts, which is why they're with us only a short while. In that time, they teach us about life, about death, about mourning, grief, joy, and above all, love.

— CHAPTER 3 —

PIECES OF HUMANITY

Hey, you. Yes, you, the one reading this book. I have a message for you: You're great. Really. Not only do you have excellent taste in books, but you're *you*. No one else is *you*. You are imbued with qualities the rest of us wish we had, with drive and emotions and lessons and wisdom. You've got a great sense of humor; some of your jokes fly right over our heads. Maybe sometimes you make a mistake; you screw something up. You know what? We all screw up. It just makes you human like the rest of us. Give yourself a break. Nobody's perfect.

We're curious creatures, aren't we? We are very good at bucking each other up. Your friend falls down; you give them a hand up, tell them it's going to be okay. How many of us do that for ourselves?

In the 1980s and '90s, there was a big drive toward trying to amplify our self-esteem, particularly in kids. It was felt that if children believed that they were special and above average, they could reach their maximum potential. What we are starting to realize is that we may have inadvertently created a generation of people who were so fixated on achieving all the external markers of success that they lost track of what could actually make them happy and successful.

To have high self-esteem, you must, to some degree at least, put yourself above others. To feel that you are great, sometimes you need to feel that others are lesser. Some people take that a step further: to feel better about themselves, they necessarily have to put others down. Many find themselves in a constant comparison war with everyone else they see. *How can I be the best if that person is better than me? I need to be even better or point out their flaws to show the world that I'm better.* That kind of behavior has narcissism written all over it, and it isn't good for individuals or those in their orbit. Social media has made this problem considerably worse: people are all encouraged to show only the best, most successful versions of themselves, and we suffer in comparison. At other times, social media users tend to "vaguebook"—posting cryptic "woe is me" statements in search of sympathy. Neither of these behaviors is healthy.

As a person in his tenth decade on this planet, I have seen a lot of these sociological and psychological changes play out. It is clear to me that most parents want what is best for their children, and that they use all available tools and wisdom to give them good lives. Those tools and wisdom are seemingly updated with each generation. Some of it works; some of it overcorrects and is pared back.

My childhood was much stricter than those of my children, my grandchildren, and now my first great-grandchild. We have mostly moved past the spanking debate, which I think is good. I really don't see how anyone can justify hitting a child. If you wouldn't hit a woman, or a teenager, how can you hit a toddler? A lot of parenting decisions are focused on language, particularly in the area of discipline. If I misbehaved as a child, I might have been told I was a bad boy. What I find fascinating is how the language in this area has been modified, for the better, I believe. It's a lesson I had to learn from my own children.

Some years ago—I don't remember the circumstances—one of my grandchildren did something messy, maybe jumped in a pile of dirt in the backyard right before dinner. "Bad girl," I said to her.

"You can't say that!" her mother told me. My other daughters nodded in agreement. What had I said? Why was I suddenly the bad guy? I had reprimanded my granddaughter, but I hadn't yelled, I hadn't been aggressive, I hadn't been physical or threatening.

"That's shaming," I was told.

This was completely new to me. I hadn't intended to shame my granddaughter; I was just trying to tell her she'd done a bad thing so she wouldn't do it again. It was here my own kids explained to me that if you tell someone they did a bad thing, you can try to teach them not to do it again; but if you make the connection that by doing a bad thing, *they themselves are bad,* it can have an impact on their sense of self-worth.

I had occasion to see an amazing TED Talk called "The Space Between Self-Esteem and Self-Compassion" from Dr. Kristin Neff. The author of *The Mindful Self-Compassion Workbook*, Dr. Neff is a pioneer in the world of teaching self-compassion—what it is, what differentiates it from self-esteem, and how to turn our innate compassion for others inward on ourselves. I reached out to Dr. Neff in preparation for this book, and she was kind enough to spend some time taking me through these concepts.

First off, Dr. Neff was able to explain to me the difference between shame and guilt—like in the example of my attempt to discipline my granddaughter for playing in the dirt. "Guilt is 'You did something bad'; shame is 'You are bad,'" she imparted. In the case of my granddaughter, a simple modification of my language to "That's bad behavior. Don't do that" is already an improvement over "Bad girl." If instead of focusing on the actions that are bad, you tell someone that *they* are bad, you stifle their capacity for emotional growth. With enough repetition, that kind of language limits someone's ability to have self-compassion, and they grow up with a decidedly negative view of themselves. They never feel good enough.

"When we feel shame, we feel like we are a failure," Dr. Neff related to me. "You feel like crawling into a hole. It shuts down your ability to learn because your mind is so overwhelmed with feelings of inadequacy. You have no space to say, 'Hmm, maybe I should try improving that. Maybe it will work out better next time if I make this change.'

"We have this superpower in our back pocket, and we don't even know it's there. Just stop and treat yourself like a friend. Just pause and say, 'Wait a second. This is hard right now. I'm not alone. How can I be kind to myself in this moment?' It's life changing."

What I found revelatory about self-compassion in my conversation with Dr. Neff is that it's based on skills we already have. I felt my mind opening with every sentence she uttered. What she was saying made a lot of logical sense. We know how to be compassionate toward others— if we're kind, understanding people (and I believe almost all of us are at our core), we do it practically every day. When your friend is going through a difficult time, your impulse is likely one of compassion: "I'm here for you. We'll get through this together." So why don't we do that for ourselves?

I have been performing for eighty-five years in one form or another. I've been in countless films, TV shows, documentaries . . . but I rarely watch myself. I don't like to see myself perform. I don't think I'm a failure, but I often find fault with the way I delivered a line or performed a particular action.

When I go to conventions, I am often asked about Captain Kirk's "Risk is our business" speech from the *Star Trek* episode "Return to Tomorrow." It's a great speech—it's all about exploration, adventure, the spirit of charting a new frontier . . . but when I think about it, I mostly remember that I flubbed part of my line. I don't recall if I wasn't supposed to say "point out" twice (once for Dr. McCoy, once for myself) or some other part of it, but I *know* that on that day, in that take, I made a mistake. I wanted another take but there wasn't time.

That was fifty-four years ago. Why does it still bother me? Why does any of it bother me? Perhaps I never learned the difference between shame and guilt. Shame can shut you down, whereas guilt can be a tool that helps you avoid hurting other people again, or yourself. Perhaps I never had it articulated to me that I could be com-passionate *to myself.* I don't blame my parents or my teachers or relatives; as I said, everyone

92

works within the conventional wisdom and tools available to them at the time.

The word *compassion* comes from the Latin words *pati*, meaning "to suffer," and *com*, which means "with." Again, simple, but it makes so much sense. *With suffering.* What is the best way to help ourselves with our suffering? Is it to feel shame, that we are not good enough? Or is it to be kind to ourselves when we experience pain? Clearly, it is the latter that will have the greatest impact on our happiness and well-being.

For some, picking up these lessons can be difficult. So much of it comes from the previous generation. I was raised in a strict household; I was pounded into the dirt at school for being a "dirty Jew." Others had abusive parents. These are difficult barriers to overcome. And yet we can remind ourselves how we would treat others who have been through that and try to turn those lessons inward. We can treat ourselves like good friends.

On February 27, 2015, one of my oldest and dearest friends, Leonard Nimoy, passed away. I have thought about him every day since; I miss him terribly. Much was made of my being unable to attend Leonard's funeral, and my decision to go ahead with a charity event in Florida instead. It was a difficult time for everyone, not least for Leonard's family. I felt my going ahead with the charity event was the right thing to do. I raised money for the Red Cross, and I spent much of the evening talking about the incredibly giving and philanthropic life my friend had led. The next year, I wrote *Leonard: My Fifty-Year Friendship with a Remarkable Man*, in which I told his rich life story and recounted our time together.

What has been hard for me to come to terms with is that the years leading up to Leonard's death had been an uneasy time in our friendship, and I have never truly understood why. Leonard and I had been friends for half a century, and over the years, we had engaged in our share of friendly spats and arguments. I still remember him ribbing me on multiple occasions while we were developing and shooting *Star Trek V*. A constant refrain was "Spock wouldn't do that," sometimes with a wink, sometimes not. When Comedy Central roasted me in 2010, I could not convince Leonard to be on the dais to participate (he did record a video introduction, which I appreciated). Our relationship had been through countless ups and downs, but this man was my brother; he was the best man at my wedding to Nerine. Our friendship had always bounced back.

In this case, however, that didn't happen. There are two possible scenarios I have gone over in my head, repeatedly. The first concerns Leonard's chronic obstructive pulmonary disease (COPD), which took his life far too early. It has been explained to me that sometimes, when one is suffering from an extreme, fatal illness, they will begin to pull back from friends and family as it gets harder to deal with their mortality. In the case of COPD, it becomes difficult to breathe, let alone talk. In my heart, I would like to believe that this played a part. I will never know for sure.

The other possibility is in some ways more baffling because of how insignificant it seemed at the time. In 2011, I was working on a documentary called *The Captains*, in which I interviewed the actors who played the captain in each iteration of *Star Trek*. I asked Leonard if he would agree to be interviewed—Spock *was* a captain in the films, after all, and Leonard was one of the reasons *Star Trek* had been so successful in capturing the hearts of audiences around the world. He declined, didn't want to be in the documentary. I was disappointed, but what could I do? If he didn't want to be in the documentary, that was that.

Part of putting together *The Captains* also involved having the documentary crew follow me around to various conventions and events. At one convention, Leonard and I had a joint appearance onstage. It started with Leonard; he left as I entered, then came back at the end, so we could finish the appearance together.

Our cinematographer was getting footage of me that day, including this appearance. He was kneeling near the stage, camera over his shoulder, and proceeded to shoot my entrance. But my entrance was also Leonard's exit, and he saw that there was a camera and assumed we were filming him against his wishes.

Backstage, Leonard was miffed. I felt he was overreacting. The camera was there to shoot me; anything with Leonard would have been incidental, and we weren't going to use it. Leonard and I had been near-lifetime friends; there wasn't any room for stupid behavior that could risk that relationship. I had no intention of trying to sneak Leonard into the film.

We left the convention without speaking again. I assumed that in time, this misunderstanding would blow over, as others had in the past. To my dismay, that never happened. I sent Leonard notes, left him messages. I felt for sure he would eventually find it in his heart to pick up the phone, so we could forgive and move on.

I cannot get back those years. I cannot unwind that minor argument to assure Leonard that I would not risk his love and friendship over some B-roll captured while making a documentary. That has been very hard.

More recently, Leonard's daughter, Julie, reached out to me and said, "He loved you, you know. He loved you." It was very kind of her to tell me that. It was so difficult for me to lose my friendship with one of the dearest people in my life, and to not have a chance to patch things up, to apologize, to make things right in any way I could. Julie Nimoy brought me a bit of peace that day.

I suppose I am now faced with a question: Can I take all of this and learn to be more compassionate toward myself? I don't know. I'm an old dog, and you know what they say about old dogs and new tricks. But I will try.

Humans are such a delicious mystery to me: we are so multifaceted and contradictory, each one of us with our foibles and eccentricities. I often wonder why we are the way we are, why we are each programmed in such different ways, cursed or blessed with different gifts.

I consider myself a reasonably educated and erudite person: I read, I discover, I seek out knowledge. Yet one day, there I was, minding my own business, and my toilet broke. I tried a few basic maneuvers, fiddled with the ball cock (yes, that's what it's called), checked that the flapper was sealed tightly, played around with the chain. I had no luck, so I called an expert.

This fellow came out to my place, and I watched in awe as he fixed the toilet. He was a very nice guy, and he fit the exact clichéd picture of a plumber. A little messy, a little unkempt, and when he bent over, you could see the crack in his ass. He seemed to work with ease as he troubleshooted the problem, replaced a requisite part, and fixed the thing up good as new.

The plumber finished up his work and presented me with a modest bill, which I was grateful to pay. As he was leaving, I stopped him.

"I have to ask," I started. "How did you know how to do that? I mean, I assume you trained and perhaps were an apprentice, but did you learn all your skills from rote, by study? Or do you look at a piece of plumbing and just naturally know your way around it?"

The plumber thought about it for a moment.

"I've never been asked that before," he said, finally. "They train you for a lot of stuff," he said. "Other things just kind of make sense." There was another pause, then he concluded: "I like how things work."

I loved that. I like how things work, too—I'm mildly obsessed—but I don't *know* how things work, and try as I might, certain things will never come naturally to me. I could write a book or direct a movie, I could recite Shakespeare and put all the correct accents in the right spots of the iambic pentameter, but I will never look at a complicated piece of machinery and just intuit how to repair it. Leonard invented the Vulcan salute, based on an old Jewish blessing, and throughout my life, no matter how much I've tried, my fingers just won't part that way; it was just a skill I wasn't blessed with. There's a scene in *Star Trek III* when I do it, but my fingers were cleverly separated with elastic.

Like I say, we are all programmed differently. Some of us are jacks-of-all-trades but masters of none; others are breathtakingly gifted in one area but very much not so in others. There are savants who can excel in amazing ways but cannot have a conversation with someone. I remember seeing a *60 Minutes* episode about an extraordinary young man named Derek Paravicini. He is a stupendously talented musician, able to recall any tune he has ever heard and play it perfectly on the piano.

Derek can change the key signature of a song at will; he can even switch between a variety of musical genres and individual composer styles as they are called out midsong. Yet when Lesley Stahl asked if he could hold up three fingers, Derek replied that he did not know how, and while he was happy for Lesley to help him demonstrate, he knew he would not be able to retain the knowledge the next time someone asked. He could not zip a zipper or button a button. He had been born three months premature and was left blind and cognitively impaired, but his aptitude for the piano was out of this world.

There have been several stories and films written about the erroneous idea that we only use 10 percent of our brains. It's a compelling concept to see what would happen if we used more, of course, but the reality is far more boring: we use 100 percent of our brain. Sometimes there are portions of our brains that are not used, but that is only in cases of brain damage or disease. We just seem to have gifts in certain areas and lack them in others; we are good at some things, and find others very difficult, even if they seem simple to almost everyone else.

A colleague of mine is a film professor. He asked me once if I would come to his university and help conduct the class. I didn't fancy myself a teacher *per se*, but he told me his students would love to pick my brain. We opened the class and gave the students a chance to hit me with questions, to ask my advice.

A hand flew into the air immediately from a young man. I called on him.

"What's your question?"

"I'm glad you picked me first," he replied. "I've written my question on my computer and it's about to die."

He asked me for some advice on filmmaking, and I gave it to him, but I had to follow up.

"Just a second . . . you're in this class every week, right?"

"Yes," he replied.

"And you knew I was coming today, and you wanted to ask me a question—that's why you wrote it down, right?"

"Yes," he said.

"Okay. You knew you were coming to class; you knew I was coming here; you prepared a question you wanted to ask . . . *and you didn't plan ahead to charge your computer?*"

Big laugh.

"I have some more advice for you," I continued. "Be fucking prepared."

Huge laugh.

If only I were joking. I mean, I *was* having fun with the lad, but it was extraordinary to me that he could be so unprepared. I went on to explain that if you want to make films, you absolutely, positively must be prepared in every aspect of the project. If you're an actor, you've got to learn your lines; if you're the director, you'd better plan for how you want to frame your shots and direct your actors; if you're in production—or just asking a filmmaker for his advice—and you need electricity, bring a generator to set, get your devices charged.

I recounted an amusing story about when I was directing a television show in Canada. There was a scene that called for us to shoot on a public street, which would be blocked off. The scene involved a gun battle. We showed up to prep and shoot the scene; the location manager came and told me we'd have to pivot to another location.

"Why?" I asked, shocked at this wrench being thrown into our plans.

"We need a permit to use guns on the street."

"And we don't have the permit?"

"I forgot to get it."

"You *forgot?*"

"We can come back here on Saturday and shoot the scene then and I'll have the permit."

Saturday morning arrives. The location manager approaches sheepishly.

"I'm so sorry. We can't shoot the scene. I forgot to get the permit, and the permit office is closed for the weekend."

If I didn't know any better, I'd have thought he was trying to sabotage the production. But that's the thing about how we're all different in our confusing humanity: something that might seem completely obvious to me was not so obvious to this guy, although it really should have been, given that it was very much in his job description. Similarly, for this fellow in the university class, it would seem so easy to ensure his computer was charged, but remembering to do so did not come naturally to him. I heard this described in a clever way: Each human is made up of certain LEGO pieces, each representing different skills. There are some LEGOs we have, and some we don't; some we have in large quantities, and others in small quantities. Since you don't need every LEGO to create something that functions in some way, when you put them together, on the surface, we're all still functional, but we have some LEGOs, and we're missing others.

I'm sympathetic to this concept, as I've been in similar situations. Sometimes people consider me aloof or oblivious to the emotions of others. Perhaps I need to be beaten over the head with something (metaphorically) before I understand what someone is trying to communicate.

In 1992, I was doing research and conducting interviews for my book *Star Trek Memories* (published the following year). I was interviewing the wonderful Nichelle Nichols (Uhura) and was dismayed to hear her tell me that she and a few of the other cast members quite disliked me while we were making the series. In their eyes, I had been cold and arrogant. I didn't make an effort to get to know them, and sometimes I would ask for story changes that I felt were critical for the success of the show, but which, unbeknownst to me, affected their screen time and the number of days they worked, and thus their paychecks.

I was horrified to learn this, ashamed that I hadn't realized it. As the lead of the series, I had been doing what I thought I was supposed to do: try with all my might to make it as good as I possibly could. I wasn't terribly social because I was obsessed with learning my lines and doing publicity for the show. I didn't realize that my efforts may have resulted in less screen time for other members of the cast. It just hadn't occurred to me.

Nichelle wasn't alone in her feelings. For *Star Trek Memories*, James Doohan (Scotty) refused my request to interview him at all, and despite my attempts to reconcile over the years, George Takei still feels sore about our association. (Walter Koenig has remained kind and understanding in his assessment of our time together, and I was honored to interview him on *Shatner's Raw Nerve* in 2011.) Toward the end of his life, Jimmy Doohan and I were finally able to mend our relationship. Backstage at one of his last conventions, I turned to him and asked, "Why were you so angry at me all these years?" Jimmy paused, then replied with a chuckle, "I don't know . . . but it must have been important!" We shared a great big belly laugh; it was a beautiful moment. I hope George and I will get there, too. But I get it—sometimes I'm off in my own world, and in the case of my fellow castmates, I didn't realize what effect that had on them. All I can think is that perhaps, like so many of us, I am missing certain LEGOs of my own.

As someone in the public eye, I try not to let other people's opinions of me—and I know they run the gamut—bother me. If you are constantly seeking the approval of others, or you're afraid to express yourself for fear of offending someone, you may find it hard to think for yourself and to make decisions.

I will say, however, in the right context, fear can be a powerful motivator. In 2014, I was asked to appear in the final four episodes of the Syfy series *Haven*. The show was shot in Nova Scotia,

Canada; the filming usually started in May and wrapped for the year by September, but this year, they were shooting two seasons back-to-back, so they had started earlier in the year and the final few episodes were shot across November and December.

That's November and December on the far east coast of Canada. Apparently, there was a debate in the writers' room as to whether sending me to Nova Scotia as winter approached might be what finally finished me off.

The best part? The studio where the show usually filmed would not be available by the time my episodes were due to be shot, which necessitated moving to another location, the only one they could find: a converted ice hockey rink. As you can imagine, ice hockey rinks are not known for their warmth.

But hey, "risk is our business," right? I decided to go for it. And it truly was colder than cold. But that frigidity had an effect on me: it focused me and gave me an incredible challenge to overcome—namely remembering my lines and ensuring my teeth didn't chatter while the camera rolled. There was a good amount of fear in taking on a challenge like that, as there can be with other things I set myself to at my age.

I know of some older actors who by virtue of their fame and experience don't feel the need to prepare as they once did. After firmly establishing himself as one of the finest actors of his generation, Marlon Brando famously decided that rather than learn his lines, he instead preferred them to be written on cue cards and left in various places around the set. He claimed it would help his spontaneity, and he became famous for these dramatic pauses (while he searched for his next line). I doubt he could have gotten away with that earlier in his career.

Some older actors will take a job, look over their lines, and say, "Just give me a few extra takes. I'll figure it out on the day." I could never do that. I fear that I wouldn't be able to "figure it out on the day." I fear not giving my best, not doing something to the absolute limit of my abilities.

In my career, I have never phoned in a job and I have always drilled my lines and prepared and analyzed each role. The day that I feel I don't want to prepare 100 percent will be the day I'll just have to pack it in. Fortunately, I cannot see that day arriving anytime soon. From a young age, I have been intoxicated by the chance to perform my craft, and to work each time at doing the best job I possibly can. That's all I've ever wanted to do, so how can I give anything less than my full self to each opportunity I agree to?

That desire I felt for performance—such that I couldn't consider anything else—is something I have seen in Seth MacFarlane. Seth grew up in Kent, Connecticut, with twin vocational aspirations: he was a talented singer but also a gifted comedy writer. "From about age five," Seth told me, "I had a laser trajectory on what I wanted to do. I wanted to be in film, and at the time, in animation."

Despite that trajectory, opportunity knocked twice simultaneously for Seth: he had to choose between a place at the Boston Conservatory of Music (to which he had been accepted) and a low-level job writing for the animators at Hanna-Barbera in Hollywood. He ultimately decided in favor of writing, and he made the move out to the West Coast.

Seth's achievements in the entertainment field have been well documented, and he has been blessed with the kind of success that has allowed him to do almost anything, including pursuing opportunities to sing. He has recorded eight albums and can sometimes be found crooning onstage at the famous Herb Alpert's Vibrato Grill & Jazz Bar.

I asked Seth what drives him. "There's a lot of self-doubt," he said. *"Did I use up my gas on the last project?* That pushes me to work harder. When you feel that way, you can either let it consume you and throw in the towel or you can use it as an engine to push yourself." I admire that Seth, as successful as he clearly is, still experiences the same kind of self-doubt as the rest of us. Despite what appears to be an impossibly vast creative output, he remains a human being, after all.

Yet he refuses to rest on his laurels. "If I'm approaching a project and it looks like something I can fail at," he further elucidated, "I'll throw myself at it even harder and take the failure if it comes. There has to be an element of fear, and that's exciting, because the possibility of failure just means that you're trying something new. I always try to make sure that exists."

Fear is something we all share, and it is in our nature that we will react differently. Fight, flight, freeze. To return to my thought at the beginning of this chapter, I believe what is most important is that we understand that we are all of us different pieces of humanity. Each of us struggles with existential concerns; we possess our individual strengths and weaknesses. But we all have a story to tell, and we all deserve a break when we hit a setback.

Not that long ago, I was at a convention, and as happens, a young boy approached me in the photograph line. He must have been about nine years old, flanked by his parents. It was obvious he was either shy or perhaps somewhere on the spectrum. The boy's father was a big, burly guy, his mother thin and delicate. The child was hesitant to make the final steps up to me for the photograph. His parents tried to encourage him. I smiled and said, "It's okay, you can come and say hello." Then, his father said to me, "Sorry about him; he's autistic."

Just like that, the child melted down. "Oh, no! No no no!" he screamed. By telling me of the boy's condition in embarrassed, apologetic tones, the father had demeaned his child, shamed him for something that was well and truly beyond his control. The boy's mother immediately tried to reassure him. "It's all right, sweetheart, it's all right." She walked away with him. I was almost in tears watching it play out in front of me. The pain that boy felt must have been awful.

I can imagine the difficulty of raising a child with special needs, and yet in that moment, I was also flabbergasted that in 2021, this boy's father seemed to feel embarrassed. Perhaps it goes back to his own childhood and the expectations that were placed on him of what it meant to be a young boy, and then a man. Did he dream of having a son who was big like him, perhaps a football player? And instead, he had a son with little physical strength? Did he think that reflected poorly on him?

The moment was upsetting on a few levels, but all I could think of was that poor boy who had been so wounded by his father's words. I don't pretend to have all the answers, but I have met many autistic kids in my life and in my work with autism charities. One boy I met described himself as "gifted with autism," and that stuck with me as a beautiful way for him to look at life. I assume it was a description bestowed upon him by his parents or through therapy, and right away, it made his condition something that was a blessing and not a curse.

After the photo session had ended, the convention folks were preparing to whisk me backstage, but I saw the boy and his parents hovering nearby, and I went over to them. "Please, please, it's okay," I told him. "I just want to say hello."

The boy perked up and looked in my direction. I asked his name and he told me.

"You know, you're strong. You're so strong. You're wonderful. I'm sorry we didn't get a chance to say hello earlier, so I want to say hello to you now. And whenever you're ready, you can say hello to me."

The boy hesitated for a few moments and replied, "Will you be back next time?" (Meaning at next year's convention.)

"Yes, I will," I replied.

"Okay," he said.

That was all he said. I made my goodbyes and told his parents what an incredible young man they were raising. Even if it was just for a moment, I hope I made a difference. I hope he went home feeling a little bit more connected, and I hope he comes back to the convention next year. I will be there waiting to see him.

— CHAPTER 4 —

IT'S ROUND. I CHECKED.

So, I went to space.

When I was first presented with this incredible opportunity—*Captain Kirk goes to space!*—I remember my reaction distinctly. "No."

I turned it down not for lack of curiosity, or because I was afraid. (Well, I *was* afraid, but that wasn't my primary motivation.) I turned it down because I'm an actor, not an astronaut. Captain Kirk was a spacefaring hero; I was a ninety-year-old performer on Medicare!

Some years back, I was on a reality series called *Better Late than Never*. The show, based on a Korean show *(Grandpas over Flowers)*, consisted of me, Henry Winkler, George Foreman, Terry Bradshaw, and Jeff Dye traveling around the world to immerse ourselves in cultures and adventures we'd never had the opportunity to experience. Essentially, it was a bucket list travel show, and boy, was it fun. The show ran two seasons and not only exposed me to incredible cultures around the world but helped me understand what a beautiful thing it can be to make new friends, especially at my age.

A short while after the series ended, the producer, Jason Ehrlich, gave me a call. I have a lot of time for Jason; he is one of the most imaginative fellows I've met, and a great producer. "Bill," Jason told me, "Jeff Bezos's company Blue Origin is going to launch soon; they're going to send civilians up into space. Bezos is going himself and will be looking for others to take with him. Wouldn't it be great if Captain Kirk went up there?"

"I don't think so," I replied. "I don't need to go into space. Besides, who on earth would be interested in an actor going up there?"

"Everybody's interested," Jason implored. "I've got some real traction on this idea."

"No," I replied politely, "I really don't think that's going to happen."

This is the thing about great producers. They're persistent. Unbeknownst to me, Jason kept up his conversations with the Blue Origin folks, and the next time he called some months later, it was to let me know that Jeff Bezos had invited me to Blue Origin's headquarters in Seattle to talk about the possibility of spaceflight. So now I was on the hook for this meeting. "Fine," I said, "I'll go. But I still can't imagine anyone is interested in sending an actor to space. Unless the idea is for me not to come back," I quipped.

Jason and I went to Blue Origin HQ. To say it's an impressive building would be an understatement. It is modern beyond belief. A few things struck me as we went through the lobby. First, *dogs*. Amazon is a very dog-friendly place to work, so it wasn't uncommon to see these wonderful little creatures scurrying around and enjoying themselves. The building even has a private dog park on the seventeenth floor for the pooches to run around.

The second thing I noticed was a section of the lobby filled with *Star Trek* paraphernalia, the centerpiece of which was a large model of the *Enterprise*. Already they've got my attention. Dogs and *Star Trek*.

Jeff Bezos joined us, and right off the bat, it was clear he was a major fan. He told me he'd grown up watching the show and spoke of the power that Gene Roddenberry's portrayal of an optimistic future had had on him as a child, as he was trying to figure out what he wanted to do in the world. We hit it off immediately. After some requisite pictures, we headed to a conference room with an unnecessarily large table, and Jason pitched his idea with all the grandeur and mystique that only a passionate producer can.

"Captain Kirk goes to space!" he declared. There was some discussion about the particulars and my place in pop culture and the beautiful synchronicity of sending the world's most famous space captain into outer space for real. There was a lot of enthusiasm in the room about the idea, which I saw was par for the course in Seattle much as it was in Hollywood. By the end of the meeting, I was genuinely excited about the prospect of being on the first civilian trip into outer space. They were still figuring out when they were going to go, and who was going to go with Jeff, so they said they'd get back to us.

As we left the meeting, Jason's excitement was palpable. "They're going to pick you," he told me. "It's going to happen." By this point, I must admit that I'd allowed myself a bit of excitement about the idea. Maybe I really was going to go into space. Soon we'd know.

Then COVID hit. Everything was delayed. More than a year went by. Finally, it was announced that Blue Origin would send four commercial astronauts into space. There was one spot left that hadn't been announced, someone Jeff Bezos would choose to accompany him.

I called Jason Ehrlich. "Do you think he'll choose me?"

"I really do," replied Jason.

Then came the announcement. Jeff had chosen his brother, Mark, to accompany him into outer space. Oh well. It's hard to compete with family.

The trip was a rousing success as the four of them made history, including world renowned aviator and Goodwill Ambassador Mary Wallace "Wally" Funk, who had become the oldest person to ever fly to space.

Then, another phone call from Jason.

"What do you think about going up on the next one?"

"Oh please, that's like asking the vice president to speak when you missed out on getting the president," I retorted.

"But Bill!" Jason kept insisting. He said he'd spoken to Bezos's people and if I was still interested, there could be room on the second flight in a couple months' time.

"No," I told him, definitively.

Then two things happened.

First, once again showing his supreme producing skills, Jason never delivered my "No" to Blue Origin. Clever guy.

Second, one evening, I found myself looking out at the sky. It was an unusually clear night, and I could really see the stars, twinkling in their time-warped majesty as their light made its way to me in Los Angeles. By some coincidence, I'd been thinking about spaceflight that day, and suddenly the stars appeared to me clearer than they'd been in years. Was this another sign from the universe? Had I turned my back on an opportunity to explore these deeper connections I'd come to believe in?

I sat there, thinking about what it might mean to go into space. To slip the surly bonds of Earth. The wonder overcame me. Then the thrill. Being weightless. Looking out into the heavens. Going where no one has gone before. (Well, where *some people* had gone before, I guess.) I also thought about the danger.

Other space disasters flooded my mind. The O-ring temperature mishap that led to the explosion of the *Challenger*; the damage caused to the wing of the *Columbia* that led to its breakup when reentering Earth's atmosphere. Other accidents, large and small, often caused by simple human error.

Thoughts of wonder had turned to thrill; thrill had now turned to fear. I became focused on human error. It's so universal. We make mistakes every day; we just don't usually have anything to do with ensuring the safety of people going into outer space! What to make of the possibility of losing your life because some well-meaning person made a mistake?

I thought long and hard about whether I really wanted to do this. Ultimately, I concluded that the wonder and thrill outweighed the fear. After all, when I had taken my family skiing so many times, my inclination had always been to start at the hardest slopes. "Don't be afraid," I would beseech them. I kept trying to get them to challenge their fears. Sometimes they got on the chairlift, made it all the way to the top . . . and then took off their skis and walked down. What did I do? I skied down, of course. Danger be damned. There was a slope to conquer.

Why did Captain Kirk hike *El Capitan* in Yosemite National Park in *Star Trek V*? "Because it's there," he declared. Because we should always be climbing for ideas, scaling the metaphorical mountains to reach greater heights. Every age should bring us to a higher level of consciousness.

And so, I thought, I must go to space. Not because I was Captain Kirk, but because I'm *alive*. Because I am here in an age in which this possibility exists, and I have been given the opportunity to experience it. Because my whole life has been about asking myself, "What can I do next? What new experience can I find? What new danger can I look right in the eye?"

I called Jason Ehrlich again. "Tell them I'll do it!"

"I already did," he replied nonchalantly. Sneaky bastard. Great producer.

I released an album last year called *Bill*, in which I collaborated with some of the finest musicians and artists in the world. A few days before the launch of Blue Origin's second commercial spaceflight, I flew to New York and met up with two of my collaborators, producer Dan Miller and lyricist/poet Rob Sharenow. They suggested that for a future album, we record a song all about my experience in outer space. We began to jot down notes about what I thought it might be like. The majesty, the wonder, the mystery. I was breathless with anticipation.

The launch itself was in a desert in Texas. Our group, consisting of me, tech mogul Glen de Vries, Blue Origin Vice President and former NASA International Space Station flight controller Audrey Powers, and former NASA engineer Dr. Chris Boshuizen, had done various simulations and training courses to prepare, but you can only prepare so much for a trip out of Earth's atmosphere! As if sensing that feeling in our group, the ground crew kept reassuring us along the way. "Everything's going to be fine. Don't worry about anything. It's all okay." *Sure, easy for them to say,* I thought. *They get to stay here on the ground.*

During our preparation, we had gone up eleven flights of the gantry to see what it would be like when the rocket was there. We were then escorted to a thick cement room with oxygen tanks. "What's this room for?" I asked casually.

"Oh, you guys will rush in here if the rocket explodes," a Blue Origin fellow responded just as casually.

Uh-huh. A safe room. Eleven stories up. In case the rocket explodes.

Well, at least they've thought of it.

Our training continued. "Should there be a problem with the rocket, the pod is equipped to eject and shoot you to a safe distance, where you will float down in a parachute." *Should there be a problem with the rocket?!* That's like when you're on a plane and they tell you that in the event of a *water landing,* your seat can be used as a flotation device. With the exception of the Miracle on the Hudson, there are very few *water landings* to speak of. Most involve the plane hitting the water at a gazillion miles an hour and exploding on impact. But just in case you land successfully on the water, they've got you covered with floating airplane seats.

The crew assured us continuously of our safety, but also did their job in articulating the immense danger we would be in at all times as we ascended against the natural forces of gravity to shove our way out of the comforts of Earth's atmosphere—and then, of course, to return.

When the day finally arrived, October 13, 2021, I couldn't get the *Hindenburg* out of my head. Not enough to cancel, of course—I hold myself to be a professional, and I was booked. The show had to go on.

We mounted those eleven flights of stairs to the top of the gantry, breathless at every stop, and got ourselves situated inside the pod, lying down in its reclining seats. Most of the practice sessions we had been through were all about how to get back into those seats for the return journey after you've been weightless. The reentry trip exposes your body to 5 g-forces, so if you didn't strap back in correctly, there was a danger that you might break your back. In the simulator, I had not been awesome at this maneuver. You have to strap yourself in in a specific order: left shoulder, right shoulder, waist, crotch, and by the time you get to the last few straps, you're lying down and can't really see where the straps are supposed to go. I didn't nail it every time, so as I sat there, waiting to take off, the importance of navigating weightlessness to get back and strap into the seat correctly was at the forefront of my mind.

That, and the *Hindenburg* crash.

Then there was a delay.

"Sorry, folks, there's a slight anomaly in the engine. It'll just be a few moments."

An anomaly in the engine?! That sounds kinda serious, doesn't it? An anomaly is something that *does not belong. What is currently in the engine that doesn't belong there?!*

More importantly, *why would they tell us that?* There is a time for unvarnished honesty. I get that. *This wasn't it.*

Apparently, the anomaly wasn't too concerning, because thirty seconds later, we were cleared for launch and the countdown began.

With all the attending noise, fire, and fury, we lifted off. I could see Earth disappearing. As we ascended, I was at once aware of pressure. Gravitational forces pulling at me. The g's. There was an instrument that told us how many g's we were experiencing. At two g's, I tried to raise my arm, and could barely do so. At three g's, I felt my face being pushed down into my seat. *I don't know how much more of this I can take,* I thought. *Will I pass out? Will my face melt into a pile of mush? How many g's can my ninety-year-old body handle?*

And then, suddenly, *relief.* No g's. Zero. Weightlessness. We were floating.

We had passed the Kármán line, sixty miles into the air, which separates Earth's atmosphere from outer space.

We got out of our harnesses and began to float around. The other folks went straight into somersaults and enjoying all the effects of weightlessness. I wanted no part in that. I wanted, *needed* to get to the window as quickly as possible to see what was out there. I pressed my face against the glass and looked down at where we'd been, where we'd come from.

The air that surrounds Earth is a very thin skin. It's sixty miles of depth, of which only about two miles, or 12,500 feet, are useful. After that, you need to have supplemental oxygen, as the atmosphere becomes too thin to fly safely without it. At sixty miles, I looked down and I could see the hole that our spaceship had punched in the thin, blue-tinged layer of oxygen around Earth. It was as if there was a wake trailing behind where we had just been, and just as soon as I'd noticed it, it disappeared.

I continued my self-guided tour and turned my head to face the other direction, to stare into space. I love the mystery of the universe. I love all the questions that have come to us over thousands of years of exploration and hypotheses. Stars exploding years ago, their light traveling to us years later; black holes absorbing energy; satellites showing us entire galaxies in areas thought to be devoid of matter entirely . . . all of that has thrilled me for years. Where matter in the universe came from, where it's going, why it's expanding . . . I know very little, but I know just enough about the universe to be in its thrall, in awe of its mystery.

I am dimly aware of the story of life on Earth, but the fascination I continue to find time and again stems from how connected all of our lives are to the fabric of our planet. Each small part of life requires synchronicity with every other part of life. There's the story of the African elephants and the termites. Termites masticate the earth around them. A colony will build a mound of nutrient-rich clay as high as six feet. Elephants will come in and rub themselves against the mound, destroying it, stamping over and eating the dust that is left behind, creating a "scar" in the ground. The rains come and fill up the hole. Then the elephants wallow in the puddle and carry away mud on their skin, making it deeper and deeper. Ultimately, it becomes a watering hole for animals all around, a whole process that began with termites. The tiniest of creatures, paving the way for the largest of creatures to create a life-nurturing watering hole for animals of all stripes.

The beauty of that single incident has been repeated billions of times over on this Earth of ours. That beauty, that magnificence of the evolutionary process, struck me so hard in that moment because when I looked in the opposite direction, into space, there was no mystery, no majestic awe to behold . . . all I saw was death.

I saw a cold, dark, black emptiness. It was unlike any blackness you can see or feel on Earth. It was deep, enveloping, all-encompassing. I turned back toward the light of home. I could see the curvature of Earth, the beige of the desert, the white of the clouds and the blue of the sky. It was life. Nurturing, sustaining, life. Mother Earth. *Gaia.* And I was leaving her.

Everything I had thought was wrong. Everything I had expected to see was wrong. Every lyric Rob and Dan and I had prewritten for my new song was wrong.

I had thought that going into space would be the ultimate catharsis of that connection I had been looking for between all living things—that being *up there* would be the next beautiful step to understanding the harmony of the universe. In the film *Contact,* when Jodie Foster's character goes to space and looks out into the heavens, she lets out an astonished whisper, "They should've sent a poet." I had a different experience, because I discovered that the beauty isn't out there, it's down here, with all of us. Leaving that behind made my connection to our tiny planet even more profound.

And it truly is *tiny*. The sun is so big, and yet it's only a moderate-sized star. We have seen images from the Hubble Space Telescope that show the true grandeur of our galaxy and more. But when I finally arrived out there, the splendor was absent. The feeling wasn't a warmth or glow that required poetry to express it; it was ominous. It was the opposite of life. And we know that: the temperature in space can get as cold as minus 455 degrees Fahrenheit. In space, you're an instant icicle; too close to the sun, an instant fireball. Every precaution we take on Earth is to ensure we are never subjected to such elements. I was so thoroughly unprepared for this experience. It was among the strongest feelings of grief I have ever encountered. The contrast between the vicious coldness of space and the warm nurturing of Earth below filled me with overwhelming sadness. Every day, we are confronted with the knowledge of further destruction of Earth at our hands: the extinction of animal species, of flora and fauna . . . things that took five billion years to evolve, and suddenly we will never see them again because of the interference of mankind. It filled me with dread. My trip to space was supposed to be a celebration; instead, it felt like a funeral.

Then, almost without warning, it was time for the return journey. I finagled my way back into my seat and we were off. Up to five g's. But this time I was not conscious of my bones feeling like iron or my face turning to mush. I was consumed with sadness.

The pod landed successfully. We had been gone for a mere ten minutes and seventeen seconds. One by one, we all made our way out of the capsule and back to *terra firma*. And from some wellspring of emotion I hadn't realized was there, I began to cry uncontrollably. The feeling was akin to being told that someone you loved has died. It was a crushing, overwhelming sadness. I was flooded with grief, unable to talk, barely able to function.

Others were popping champagne corks, yahooing, slapping each other with high fives. Every time some particle of champagne hit my arm, it was like a hot iron. It was the antithesis of everything I was feeling.

Jeff Bezos came by with a camera crew and interviewed me. I must have sounded nonsensical as I tried to process what I was feeling. I told him, "I hope I never recover from this." I knew that what I was feeling was something I will carry with me for the rest of my life, something I must share with as many people as I can. Going into space made me so aware of how fragile our lives are here on Earth, how we *need* each other, and need to continue to strengthen the bonds that connect us to each other. Because out there, there is no life. There is no *us*.

It took me some time to process the over-whelming feeling of grief that had confronted me in space. When I was eighteen years old, I had hitchhiked across America from the East Coast to Los Angeles, down to San Diego, up to Vancouver, and back across Canada to home in Montreal. It had taken me a month to "thumb" my way across the North American continent and back again. I have traversed the United States on a motorcycle, which took closer to five days. I've driven cross-country with a baby, with children, with a dog, and alone. Each time, I was confronted by the seemingly boundless stretches of *nothing*—as if the roads in front of me went on for infinity. Earth seemed endless. Yet from space, I could measure the circumference of Earth—this place in which all life as we know it resides—with just a short trace of my finger. That's how insignificant we are in the scheme of the universe.

I liken it to a moment I experienced in 2017, when I was in Cambridge Cathedral at King's College filming a documentary. At one point,

I sat on a pew and looked up, where the sun was streaming through the ornate stained-glass windows. Elsewhere, someone was cleaning the great organ, and alternating between polishing pipes and playing thunderous chords from a piece by Bach. As this haunting music filled the cathedral, I caught sight of a tiny mote of dust, visible only because of where the sun had caught it at this particular time of day. I thought to myself, *Wow. In the grandeur of the universe, that must be what Earth must look like.* That is what reverberated in my mind in the days and weeks after my return to Earth. Our planet is an insignificant grain of sand in an immeasurable desert, and we are the microscopic life-forms on that piece of sand.

I learned later that I was not alone in this feeling. It is called the "Overview Effect" and is not uncommon among astronauts, including Yuri Gagarin, Michael Collins, Sally Ride, and many others. Essentially, when someone travels to space and views Earth from orbit, a sense of the planet's fragility takes hold in an ineffable, instinctive manner. Author Frank White first coined the term in 1987: "There are no borders or boundaries on our planet except those that we create in our minds or through human behaviors. All the ideas and concepts that divide us when we are on the surface begin to fade from orbit and the moon. The result is a shift in worldview, and in identity." It can change the way we look at the planet but also other things like countries, ethnicities, religions; it can prompt an instant reevaluation of our shared harmony and a shift in focus to all the wonderful things we have in common instead of what makes us different. It reinforced tenfold my own view on the power of our beautiful, mysterious collective human entanglement, and eventually, it returned a feeling of hope to my heart. In this insignificance we share, we have one gift that other species perhaps do not: we are *aware*—not only of our insignificance, but the grandeur around us that *makes* us insignificant. That allows us perhaps a chance to rededicate ourselves to our planet, to each other, to life and love all around us. If we seize that chance.

In a subsequent conversation with Jeff Bezos, I related to him the sadness that met me and that I had carried around. I wept for our planet, for the generations that will likely be greeted by ever-worsening environmental disasters that we have helped cause.

Then Jeff let me in on his plan.

Jeff Bezos, I must say, is a misunderstood person. His excursion into outer space seems, on the surface, to be the excesses of capitalism shown off in a gaudy display of ego, and yet ego is not what has driven Jeff to space. He is a deeply thoughtful man who has been shaped by his own experiences and upbringing, the same as all of us, hiding behind whatever mask he has to don each day to go out into the world.

Jeff's mother was seventeen and still in high school when she gave birth to him. His maternal grandparents were very involved in his life, and he loved and idolized them, especially his grandmother. One day, when Jeff was ten, he was in the back seat of his grandparents' car on a summer road trip somewhere. Jeff's grandmother was a persistent smoker, and the wafting of cigarette smoke riled this precocious young boy. Ever eager to show off his advanced arithmetic skills, Jeff started running calculations.

"You really ought to stop smoking," Jeff told his grandmother.

"I know, I know," she replied, taking another drag. Jeff's grandmother knew intellectually that smoking was likely killing her, but she had an addiction and no way to break it, so it was a sensitive subject for her.

Thinking he was just the cleverest person in the car, Jeff turned to his arithmetic. "If every cigarette took three minutes off your life, and you smoke three packs a day . . . Grandma, you've taken nine years off your life!"

Jeff thought he was very smart for coming up with this calculation, but his grandmother found herself weeping uncontrollably. She *knew* cigarettes were killing her, but it wasn't that simple for her to quit. It was like a long suicide note she couldn't stop herself from writing.

Jeff's grandfather stopped the car, got out, and indicated for Jeff to join him. Jeff obeyed. His grandfather put his hands on Jeff's face and said, surprisingly calmly, given what had just transpired, "Jeffrey, it's so much easier to be clever than it is to be kind." With that, Grandpa went back to the driver's side of the car and got back in. Jeff stood in stunned silence. "I have never forgotten that moment," he told me.

It is that lesson that continues to resonate with Jeff. He will freely admit that he doesn't always get every decision right, but his heart is in the right place. He gave me some insight into his grand plan for outer space. He wants to send polluting industries up there.

Up there.

There has been some talk about what the next phase of space exploration can do. Some have suggested we colonize Mars or put a base on the moon. What Jeff wants to do is help our planet by removing some of the heavy polluting industries that are choking it. If this were even possible, I suggested, surely it must be met by also continuing to find ways to reduce the impact of those industries or eliminate some of them altogether. And certainly, that is part of the future that Jeff sees. For right now, he believes that he has the technology to make his part of the plan a reality. To send polluting industries up 280 miles into a geocentric orbit so they can generate what they need to generate but send the pollution into the vastness of space.

Now, we've kind of heard this story before throughout Earth's history. "Just dump all of that garbage into the ocean. It's so big, it won't be a problem." Until it became a problem. If we are able to move polluting industries into outer space, will they pollute space? We already know there are occasionally issues with *space junk* messing with the International Space Station or crashing to Earth. However, I can attest that there is just so much space out there, that maybe Jeff might be onto something. Ideally, long before there is enough space pollution to worry about, we will have figured out a way to continue Earth's industrialization without also harming our precious planet.

I was outwardly skeptical at what Jeff was suggesting, no matter how altruistic his goals may be. "What you're describing might take a hundred years," I exclaimed. "We don't have a hundred years. We might have ten."

Jeff paused, and then, in a line that would make Gene Roddenberry proud, he intoned, "Without hope, you have nothing. You've always got to have hope."

In a heartbreaking footnote to my experience going to outer space, on November 11, 2021, Jeff

Bezos called me with terrible news: our fellow traveler Glen de Vries had died in a plane crash. He was piloting a small plane, as he (and as I) had done countless times before, but something had evidently gone wrong, and he and his friend Thomas Fischer crashed in a small town in New Jersey. Glen was an entrepreneur and philanthropist and a wonderful, soulful human being. I only knew him a short while, but he always brought a smile to everyone's face. Going to space was a dream for Glen; even though he passed away far too soon, I am glad he was able to realize his dream. We are on Earth for such a whisper of a moment. The right time to seize the day and reach for the stars was, is, and forever will be now. Glen de Vries was the embodiment of that message. May he rest in peace.

— CHAPTER 5 —

LISTEN TO THE MUSIC

I've recorded eight albums, from my original experimental opus, *The Transformed Man*, to the recently released (and critically acclaimed!) autobiographical *Bill*. The reviews run the gamut from the lowest of the low to the highest of the high. The biggest question my work has seemed to provoke, especially back in the original "Mr. Tambourine Man" days, is "Is he serious?"

You see, if I was in on the joke, then I must have been some sort of master of satire. If I was serious, *What was I thinking?!* That question has continued to be asked. *The Transformed Man* has, to my delight, enjoyed something of a critical reappraisal. One critic compared it to the style Andy Kaufman made famous in the late 1970s and described the album as a "must hear, (unintentional?) comedy classic."

So here, in 2022, at the age of ninety-one, I will answer the question: Was I doing Andy Kaufman, or was I serious?

My dear readers, I was serious. If anything, Andy Kaufman was doing *me!*

But wait—that doesn't mean I was crazy. Hear

me out; oh, please hear me out! Why won't you hear me out?

As always, to understand my motivations, we must return to my childhood in Montreal.

A lot of musicians begin their journeys through song and composition after hearing lush soundscapes at a young age and then developing the desire to create their own. I had a similar experience, but it took hold much later than most.

As a child, I did not have music. You might ask how that is possible. Isn't music everywhere? Didn't young kids rock out in their own contemporary fashion? Perhaps they did, but not in my home.

My home did not sing. The walls did not echo with the reverberations of records making their circular journey at 33⅓ revolutions per minute (or, way back in my day, 78 revolutions per minute). Quite simply, nobody played music. Nobody played Sinatra. Nobody played the big band records of the day.

The only music in the house would be the Metropolitan Opera on the radio. We would hear it every Saturday afternoon. My father worked Monday to Friday and Saturday mornings; when he returned on Saturday afternoon, he'd walk into the living room, tune the radio on low volume to the Metropolitan Opera radio broadcast, and lie down on the couch for a much-needed nap.

That was the only music that entered our home.

I would sit on the floor by my father, and I would listen. I didn't know the names of the songs; I didn't know what they were singing about; I had no understanding whatsoever of orchestration or the nuances of performance. All I knew was that when I heard some great melodic line in an opera, I loved it.

Though my exposure to music was clearly limited, there were cracks in the wall; light was beginning to shine in and give me the chance to broaden my nascent interest in this art form. As a teenager, I became captivated by the performances of a burlesque dancer named Lili St. Cyr (born Willis Marie Van Schaack). She would perform at the Gayety Theatre in the heart of Montreal's red-light district. Some of my schoolmates and I would take the streetcar down to Sainte-Catherine Street on a Friday afternoon to watch Lili St. Cyr and the racy, bawdy burlesque revues of the time.

Make no mistake, I was there to see Lili. She was sex on legs. But I would stay at the theater and marvel at the incredible night's entertainment. There were hilarious comedians, titillating dance numbers, and music. Oh, the music. Brass bands, violinists, and singers who seemed to have some boundless energy stored up just for a Friday-night gig. People sang and danced and jumped around, and I got right in on the act. It was eye- and ear-opening at the same time. I wanted more.

When I got to university, I was finally exposed to the full cornucopia of aural pleasures. A classmate would play a record. I had my own radio and could tune the dial to whichever station pleased me. I was liberated. I was enthralled by sound. By music. Not only that, but I had an outlet to express and experiment with my newfound infatuation.

At McGill University, I thrived in the performing arts. For three years, I wrote, directed, acted, and even sang (sometimes all four) in the college musicals, which were known as the "Red, White and Blue." During my senior year, I had a little office underneath a staircase in the student lounge, where I could meet with my fellow actors to work on whatever performance was upcoming. It was a totally private space, and if I wanted to, I could go there solo, just to think, to daydream, and to listen to the radio.

In this little office, nestled away with my thoughts and my radio, something became clear to me: I adored music, but I had no idea how to *make* music.

Well, that had to change. Challenge, meet Bill Shatner.

Never one to half-ass any challenge, I set myself to becoming an expert. I borrowed library books on musical theory: staves, notes, chords.

I bought an acoustic guitar and also carried a fretboard with me to try to learn fingering and how to play. Sadly, I wasn't very good.

But what about my voice? Perhaps this was an instrument I could truly make sing. I practiced in the place with the best acoustics, as many of us do: the shower.

A few years after university, I was living in New York with my wife Gloria and was beginning to have some success on Broadway and in television. My foray into music would have to wait, and, ironically, it wasn't until we moved from New York and Broadway to Los Angeles and television that I undertook to study and work on my singing.

I found a local singing coach and began to take voice lessons, learning almost instantly that I didn't have perfect pitch. I discovered, however, that with enough practice, one can develop relative pitch.

By this point, it was the early 1960s. Gloria and I were raising our first two children, Leslie and Lisabeth. Following my adoption of Morgan from the Rancho Dobe kennel, I had concluded that for a dog to truly be happy, it needed a companion, so we bought a second Doberman, whom I named Strathcona, after Strathcona Academy in Outremont, Quebec. My career was on the rise and my home was blessed with a wife, two incredible daughters, and two loyal pets. All seemed well on the surface, but all was not well.

Gloria and I had followed all the steps of what we thought marriage was supposed to be, but a distance had grown between us. It had first become apparent to me years earlier, when we'd made the four-day drive from New York to LA and barely said a word to each other. Not because we were fighting, but rather because we had seemingly run out of conversation. This was a warning sign, but one that neither of us heeded.

Life in Los Angeles was good, and getting better, but Gloria was troubled. In the late 1950s, the concept of mental health was still in its medical and academic infancy; we didn't know what we know now—that Gloria had a chemical imbalance. Without a diagnosis or even a common frame of reference, she just seemed a little *off,* which was difficult for me and her friends and family to comprehend; it must have been torture for her.

Little things started to bother Gloria in out-size ways. The most painful for me was that she'd somehow decided that the clicking of our dogs' nails on the floor as they walked was too much for her. "You can keep one," she told me. I was flabbergasted. These dogs were like children to me (and they were great with our *actual* children), and I was being made to get rid of one on the absurd premise that *one* dog's nails tapping on the floor was acceptable, but *two* dogs' nails tapping on the floor simply could no longer be tolerated.

I was devastated, not just for myself, but for Morgan and Strathcona, who would not have any way of rationalizing why they were being split up. I felt the best thing I could do was to give one of the dogs to a friendly home—ideally somewhere I could visit. I asked my singing teacher if he would like to adopt Strathcona, and he was only too happy to take him in. Every time I went for a lesson, I was reunited with my former companion. That was heaven. But leaving was hell. Strathcona would howl in pain when I left. Instead of being welcome reunions, my visits to the singing coach's house took on a certain agony—more and more it felt like I had given up one of my children.

Eventually, the pain of those visits became too much, and I decided the best thing I could do for the dog (and myself) was to stop going to those singing lessons. My interest in singing had become too wrapped up in memories of Strathcona, and so, I gave it up. To this day, I still feel the pain of giving up that beautiful dog.

In 1968, while I was shooting *Star Trek*, a Decca Records producer got in touch with me to ask if I'd be interested in recording an album.

"What a great idea!" I told him. "I've always wanted to do an album." There was only one problem, I admitted: I couldn't sing. I wanted to, so earnestly. How I wanted to hold long, sustained notes and sing like an angel, to have one of those voices that can make music in a way that no other instrument can.

I don't remember if the Decca producer complimented my command of the spoken word, or if inspiration struck me directly, but it was agreed that we could produce some sort of nontraditional album. That excited me a great deal.

I went away and thought about what kind of album this might be. During my years in regional theater, the Stratford Festival, and Broadway, I had become competent in poetry and verse; I had taken a special interest in the rhythm of poetry, the onomatopoeia of words, the metrical feet trochaic, iambic, anapestic, and dactylic. I was a good reader of Shakespeare; I could handle his words and his poetry. I loved reading it out loud purely for the sound, the language . . . and what I felt was the *music* of it all. There was something there, a concept: What if I could combine great literature with music? We could find songs that matched the philosophy of the literature and meld them, segue from one song to another, and in doing so, tell a story, offer commentary.

Unfortunately, even that minimal description I just gave is a far more advanced and considered version than I was able to articulate in

1968, and the contemporary reviews bore that out.

In my other albums, produced decades later, I would come to refine this idea and, in my humble opinion, finally achieve the concept I'd been grasping at way back then.

But it had all come from a very earnest place. I was serious. I knew what I was trying to do. I was on the verge of a new kind of performance art. Perhaps I was on the verge of idiocy. All I know is that when I made the album, I longed to express myself in music. Some say that's exactly what I did. I'll let you be the judge.

The Transformed Man came together in a somewhat slapdash fashion. I was on set one day and chatting with our dolly pusher, Cliff Ralke. I mentioned that Decca wanted me to make this album. "The concept is pretty neat," I offered. "I'll speak poetry to music and we'll put music to poetry. It'll be great."

Cliff's eyes lit up. "You know, I'm really into music, and my father's a music producer. Why don't we do the album together?"

So that became the team that begat *The Transformed Man*. Cliff's father, Don Ralke, wrote the music, I performed the poetry and spoken-word covers of hit songs, and we blended them all into what I thought was a modern and exciting concept.

The time neared when the album was due to

"drop." (I don't think we said that in the 1960s, but I do try to keep up with my modern musical parlance.) I was booked on *The Tonight Show* with Johnny Carson to promote the album. It was decided that I'd perform the second track from the album, "Theme from *Cyrano*," and then lead into my recitation of Bob Dylan's 1965 hit, "Mr. Tambourine Man." The conceptualization of this mash-up (see—told you I'm always keeping up with the lingo) was that an addict was unable to survive without his drugs. The segue from *Cyrano*'s "I will climb perhaps to no great height, but I will climb alone" into what most thought was Bob Dylan's take on LSD seemed perfect, and we had a lot of fun putting it together in the studio. I felt it was a great way to introduce a television and live studio audience to the concept of the album.

I rehearsed with the band and felt good about how the performance was going to turn out.

Shortly before the show started, Johnny's producer Fred de Cordova approached me. "Bill, the song you've rehearsed is six minutes long, but we only have three minutes in your segment. What do you want to do, the literature piece or the song?"

This momentous decision changed my life. It would just take thirty years to do so.

"I'll do the song," I said.

Now, you must understand that on the album,

Cyrano's speech builds to Dylan's song. It is there to project the confidence of a man who wants to believe he does not need drugs, and it ramps up from zero to ten, only to hit the peak of ecstasy and agony in "Mr. Tambourine Man," where it all comes crashing down. But on *The Tonight Show*, I didn't have that lead-in. I had to start at an eleven and descend straight into the addict's madness. Without the ramp-up, that madness came across like, well, *madness.*

It was a disaster. No one had any idea what I was doing. I even caught in my peripheral vision Johnny mouthing "What the fuck!?" to Fred.

My music career was a joke. I was finished; dead and buried. I'd never make music again.

Or would I? Here again, it feels like the universe had a plan. That each failure was just a door to a later success. If I could just be open to it, I would find a connection from one journey to the next. Little did I know that *The Transformed Man* would have a lasting effect on a young musician who found it unwanted in a bin at a yard sale in North Carolina. A person I had most assuredly never heard of then, or even when he came into my life in the late 1990s.

My agent sent me a letter. It had been delivered by a highly successful recording label on behalf of their client, a musician who said he had found my album at a young age and had written a song for me that he felt was well suited to my style of musical performance. The letter closed with a request: Would I go into a recording studio with him and record it?

I called my youngest daughter. After the usual chitchat, I got down to business.

"Melanie," I entreated, "who is Ben Folds?"

"Are you serious?" she deadpanned in reply.

"Yes," I countered innocently. "My agent gave me a letter from him; it seems he's a musician of some kind?"

"Dad," Melanie advised, with that "Dad" tone that only daughters possess, "I know you haven't listened to any new music since Neil Diamond, but Ben Folds is one of the best, most popular musicians in the world. His band is called Ben Folds Five."

"Oh, like a jazz group," I guessed.

"No, their music is . . . well, it's everything. It's amazing. You have to listen to it."

"Okay, I will," I relented. "So, there are five of them, right?"

"No, there are three."

"Then why are they called Ben Folds Five?"

"Because they're quirky. Just . . . just listen to the music," she told me.

Then there was a pause. Melanie's voice turned inquisitive.

"Wait a second. Let's go back a few steps," she said. "You said he wrote you a letter?"

I elucidated the contents of the letter: that this

Ben Folds fellow had acquired a copy of *The Transformed Man* at a yard sale when he was younger and loved it. He wrote a song for me and wanted me to record it with him.

Melanie was flabbergasted. "You have to do it," she said. It was clear that she simply would not take no for an answer.

The good news is, I had no intention of saying no. That's the opposite of my philosophy; plus, if someone was a fan of *The Transformed Man* and really understood what I was trying to do, how could I refuse them?

So, I did the song. It was called "In Love" and appeared on Ben's experimental spin-off project *Fear of Pop: Volume 1*, released in 1998. I adored the song Ben wrote for me, and though I didn't know it at the time, that simple act of Ben reaching out to me would begin a beautiful reawakening of my career as a recording artist.

What had started as a failure in 1968 with *The Transformed Man* turned into a wonderful renaissance thirty years later, and all because, somehow, that original album of mine reached the right person.

During the writing of this book, I reached out to Ben to hear his side of the story; what possessed him at the height of his fame and success to contact me. Here's Ben's recollection of the affair:

I loved *The Transformed Man* as a kid. Independently of any of the specific songs, independently of what I knew of you from television. I just really liked the record. And when I like a record, I fucking like the record! So, when I was a kid, I listened to it a whole lot. And as I got older, I realized that there might be some reason that the record would be somehow ironic to older people, and they'd think it was funny, that you were just doing music in a funny way, but I could never hear it that way. All I ever heard was someone performing the songs in a way that just kind of captivated me— because everyone's talking at you all the time, but not many people have a voice that makes you really listen.

Based on that, I wrote a letter. I was really young. I sent it to the William Morris Agency or some other connection that might reach you. I was in high school and I wrote a song for you and wrote you a letter. I got a form letter back from the agency. Years later, when I had a hit, I sent the letter again along with a formal request from my record label. Now I'm all grown up and it was like, "Now can we do the song?" And you said yes!

Interestingly, while you were on your

way to the studio, I was going through the song, and I realized that the song was written about a high school kid, with a high school kid's ability. It was terrible. It was a shitty song. So, I wrote a whole new song before you showed up.

That was the first time I'd learned that Ben had rewritten the song. I remember recording it, and it was incredible. I truly had my eyes opened to what was possible musically for me to achieve; I just needed a genius like Ben Folds to show me the way. I had such a wonderful time with him laying down that track, as the kids say. We even got to perform it together on *Late Night* with Conan O'Brien.

A few years later, Ben and I collaborated on the album *Has Been*. *Has Been* was an utter delight for me, and it gave me real confidence that what I had been trying to do all those years ago—to marry spoken-word lyrics, experimental concepts, sound effects, and lush music—was, at last, possible. Our breakout single, a cover of Pulp's "Common People," was a big hit, and the album charted on *Billboard*.

Making *Has Been* with Ben was quite an experience. I flew to Nashville, so we could write and record the album. The first day's session was due to begin at 11 a.m. in a recording studio near Ben's house. I was raised in the theater and in broadcast television. When your call time is 11 a.m., you're there absolutely no later than 11 a.m. I arrived at 10:55 a.m. and waited.

And waited.

And waited.

Finally, a little after 11:30, in strolled Ben Folds. He greeted me and walked me into the recording studio.

"I'm sorry," I told him, "I thought we were supposed to meet at 11 a.m."

"Yeah," he replied nonchalantly.

"Well," I said, somewhat pointedly, "you're half an hour late."

"Yeah," acknowledged Ben, again casually.

Okay, I thought; I don't want things to get off on the wrong foot. Let's get into it.

"What's the plan?" I asked him.

"I don't know," Ben responded.

"You don't know?"

"I think I'll just noodle around on the piano."

This wasn't how I was accustomed to working.

"Where's the design? Do you have notes? A one-two-three-four of how you want this to go?"

"No, no, no," Ben said, "we're just going to noodle around and see what happens."

You've heard of an unstoppable force meeting an immovable object? This was the discipline of making movies smashing into the haphazardness of making music.

We compromised. There would not be any set

formula for how we would work, but by gum, if we said we'd start at 11 a.m., *we would both be there* at 11 a.m.

Watching Ben create music is mesmerizing. He has a method of figuring his way around a melody or theme until he's satisfied. As he told me, "Until they pry it from our cold dead hands, we can always do better."

I asked my friend Seth MacFarlane about the art of composition. Over the years, Seth has cultivated a relationship with movie maestro John Williams, and told me he has peppered Williams repeatedly with questions about his process.

The "secret sauce," Seth posited, is that the true genius of the best composers, be they film composers like John Williams, Max Steiner, or Jerry Goldsmith, or song composers and arrangers like Nelson Riddle, Gordon Jenkins, and Johnny Mandel, is that they know what to write and what *not* to write. "If you look at a piece of score by Nelson Riddle or John Williams or any one of these masters," Seth told me, "it's surprising how much blank space there is." He mused that the best composers are true storytellers, and what he was saying made a lot of sense to me. As actors, our storytelling often relies on *beats* or pauses. (Some say I have . . . my own . . . style . . . of pausing.) Sometimes it is the gaps in the expression of a thought or idea that allow that idea to be its most compelling. When I thought back to my experiences with Ben Folds, I could remember him, perhaps unconsciously, looking for those gaps, those pauses . . . searching to find the best way of telling the story of each song.

A quick aside: Ben later told me that he'd been warned by someone at the studio that he needed to be very careful in how he directed me. The exact phrase he was told was that "Shatner eats directors for breakfast." Ben was scared initially but dismissed the warning, since directing me was exactly what he was there to do.

I hadn't realized that perception of me was out there, but I think it could be traced back to two incidents that were made public (thanks, Howard Stern!), thus allowing it to take hold.

One of these incidents occurred when I was recording some introductory lines for a radio special. I'm not even certain there was a director there; I think the fellow directing me was likely the engineer. We did the first take. I thought it was pretty good; right off the bat, the engineer came back with notes: he wanted more *excitement*.

"It sounded super laid back," he said. I'd like to think that I'd been doing this long enough to know how to get it right, but I'm not allergic to feedback, so I turned up the excitement in the second take. Better?

"Uhh, ummm," came the response, demonstrating the engineer's lack of satisfaction. I asked him to read the line for me (something most actors really don't like) so I could understand what he was asking for. He read the line and, bless him, it was clear he wasn't a performer. It was pretty clunky. But hey, they were paying me to be there, and this was the guy they'd asked to capture my performance, so I guessed I should give him what he wanted.

For take three, I parroted the line back to him as exactly as I could, trying to hit all the same beats and dynamics he had given me. He didn't like it. In fact, he thought I was making fun of him. I told him, no, I was doing what he'd asked. "If you've brought me in and you don't like how I'm performing and you have a better version, then I will listen to each line and repeat it exactly as you wish," I explained. Suddenly, the engineer was backtracking; on reflection, now he *liked* my first take!

I probably had a little fun at his expense by going on with it as long as I did, as he was clearly getting more uncomfortable by the second, but in my defense, if you're going to call an actor's performance "super laid back" after the very first take, you'd better have a very clear understanding of what you want and a plan for how to communicate it.

The other incident goes back years earlier but made its way onto the internet (as things often do) at a later date. We were recording lines for the computer game *Star Trek: Judgment Rites*, the

1993 follow-up to the acclaimed *Star Trek: 25th Anniversary*. It was the last time that the entire original cast of *Star Trek* appeared together, although we mostly recorded our lines separately.

I am not particularly adept with technology, but I remember being so impressed with the stories for both *25th Anniversary* and *Judgment Rites*. The games played as if they were episodes of the series, so each level was like a contained adventure. I am told by those who played both games that they were fun and joyful; they're now considered "abandonware" online, so if you never got a chance to play them, see if you can go online and find an old version that is playable on your modern systems. I think you'll enjoy yourself, as the games really do capture the exciting spirit of the original series.

This case of my allegedly eating a director for breakfast came down to the pronunciation of a word within one of Captain Kirk's lines. The line is "Spock, sabotage the system."

Whether it was my French-Canadian Québécois influence or just a particular pronunciation that somehow stuck with me, I have always pronounced the word *sabotage* with an *aa* sound on 'tage,' like *apple*. (As a general rule of thumb, I happen to subscribe to the axiom that you should never make fun of someone for mispronouncing a word, as it likely means they learned it by reading, and that should always be applauded.)

The director wanted me to say *sabo-tahge* (with an *ah* sound like, ironically, the French *fromage*).

"I don't say *sabo-tahge*," I explained. "*You* say *sabo-tahge;* I say sabo-*taaj*." I wasn't arguing that one was more valid than the other; some folks say *nee*-ther, others say *nigh*-ther. I happen to say *sabo-taaj;* if you look back at my career, anytime that word comes up in any of my performances, I am consistent in how I pronounce it.

The director and I went back and forth a little, but it certainly wasn't a big deal. The point is—and I promise, there is one—I don't eat directors for breakfast, to which Ben can attest. You'd just better know what you want from me when I come in, and, more importantly, don't ask me to pronounce sabo-*taaj* as sabo-*tahge*. I simply won't do it. For you see, it would sabotage my natural Shatnerian pronunciation.

The highlight of my musical relationship with Ben Folds came in late 2004. Ben was performing a sold-out show at the El Rey Theater, a beautiful, historic art deco venue in Los Angeles. Toward the end of the show, Ben brought out the magnificent Joe Jack and yours truly for a few numbers. The audience was a little baffled, to be sure, but they seemed content enough to give me a chance. Some of them, I presume, had listened to our *Has Been* album, which had been released a few weeks earlier, so it wasn't entirely shocking for Ben to have invited me onto the stage with him.

We opened with "Has Been" and played through a number of songs from the album; each successive song brought the audience further along with us. I could feel their attitudes changing, from humoring me (and Ben for bringing me up onstage) to starting to dig what they were hearing. "Common People" really got their engines revving.

The true moment of wonder, however, came at the end. We had discussed whether I should dip my toe back into the waters of *The Transformed Man*—that misunderstood and maligned original experiment. Ben told me to go for it. Borrowing some of his confidence, I threw caution to the wind, and we rocked out with "Lucy in the Sky with Diamonds." The audience, confused at first by my presence, had quickly become converts. They ate it up.

At the end of the song, per a suggestion Ben had made in rehearsal, I thrust my middle finger into the air triumphantly. I was at once basking in the glow of the crowd's rapturous reaction and also, in my mind, casting off the demons of the contemporary critical collapse of *The Transformed Man* thirty-six years earlier.

The crowd went bananas.

We left the stage and, still, they bellowed. They wanted more. "One more song!" they cried. But we didn't have anything else. The backstage folks ushered us toward the stage door and to a waiting car. From the alley out back, I could still hear the audience. My daughter Lisabeth recalls that even once the house lights came up, the crowd still wanted me to come back to the stage: "I have a really vivid memory of that night. It was one of the most amazing moments I think I ever saw in a performance, because an audience that had come to hear Ben Folds was suddenly watching William Shatner. They did not know what to expect, and certainly didn't expect to be motivated by it. But within two to three minutes, you could see them changing their minds; they were cheering and yelling and screaming. It was the most enthusiastic audience I think I've ever seen, short of a Bruce Springsteen concert back in the heyday of Bruce Springsteen."

I wish that I'd had another song to perform. (Maybe we should have added "Mr. Tambourine Man" to our repertoire!) But I was whisked away. I swear, I could still hear the thundering of feet on the floor of the El Rey and the cacophony of cheers as the car swept me away in the night. It was truly one of the highlights of my life, and I owe it all to Ben Folds.

Has Been allowed me an opportunity I hadn't had since 1968: to perform music. With each album, I developed my unique spoken-word style. When Ben and I had collaborated on our

155

album, he'd told me, "Just write the truth. I'll come up with the music." In my own way, that is what I've tried to do with each successive album. Some songs are fun and lighthearted, others are serious meditations on the world; as always, however, I try not to take myself too seriously, as I know I'm not the next incarnation of Leonard Cohen.

Developing this style of music that I was not quite successful in pulling together back on *The Transformed Man* has opened so many doors for me. I've performed a spoken-word poetry version of Sarah Palin's tweets (perhaps the only way to understand them) on *The Tonight Show* with Conan O'Brien; I've collaborated with genius recording artists; I've sung CeeLo Green's "Fuck You" *twice* on television—first on *Lopez Tonight* and again many years later on *Better Late than Never*, where I think I understood it and performed it better, but I believe it may have been cut for time in most broadcasts.

For all of this, I must thank Ben Folds and all of you. Actors can act and singers can sing only if they are compelled to do so, either by some force inside them, or a willing audience, or both. You have been that audience, and for that I will always be grateful. I look at my music career as a gift—it is bestowed on me by folks like yourself who are willing to listen to my albums and enjoy the journey with me.

What has long fascinated me about music itself is the way it can connect us to each other. From the earliest days of tribal music, of people *literally* figuring out how to create pleasing sounds, all the way to the songs and arrangements that find their ways into our souls, music *communicates.* It is there in our deepest connections to each other and the universe: church choirs, wedding bells, the blowing of the shofar, the Islamic call to prayer. It is even there in our very language: something was *orchestrated;* we must carry out this act in *concert* with some other group; we were *in harmony.*

Music binds us to each other. How many of you have bonded with your partners over their love of a particular band or artist or style of music? Not only can music bring us together, but it can penetrate our minds and souls in a way that even the most beautiful and powerful of words cannot. Ben Folds took the concept even further when I discussed it with him. "We are wired for music," he told me, and he was being quite literal. Scientists have studied the effects of sounds on the brain. When we're exposed to speech, or in conversation, two areas of the brain—the Broca's Area and the temporal lobe's auditory cortex—light up. (The frontal lobe's motor cortex also lights up when we speak in response.) But when we hear music, nearly the whole brain lights up.

Ben explained: "Music is the hijacking of one

of the most intense ways of survival and interest that we have in our life." He calls these "sound stories."

If you think about it, our brain's understanding of sound fires on so many different levels. Ben explained it to me this way: "Let's say you live in a house. You're lying in your bed. You hear a sound outside: someone *dragging* something, like a trash can. Within only one or two steps of the dragging of this can, you are flooded with information: you can tell which direction it's going, how fast it's going. You can make emotional assumptions based on speed and effort, or the rhythm of this simple act of dragging a trash can. The person might be in a hurry, they might be irritated, cold, angry, drunk. All these assumptions—and they're often correct—from just a soundscape, the briefest *sound story*. If someone speeds up, the pitch of that sound story changes; if they're moving away from you, the frequency of the sound changes, its pitch decreases, the pressure of the sound on your brain drops as the trash can fades into the distance. These sounds, this music of life, is telling us a story. Every time."

These sound stories are the beginning of a connection we form and use to communicate. Some might say that there is a difference between *hearing* music and *feeling* music. I agree with this: even though it may be difficult to articulate, somehow, we *know* when we are feeling a piece of music. It hits us in a deeper spot than merely listening to something does. I put this to Ben and, naturally, he took it even further: "First we *detect* music, then perhaps we hear it, then we listen to it, and finally, if everything aligns the right way for us, we let it in and we *feel* that music."

I want you, dear reader, to think about your own reactions to music. Have you ever been in a position where you heard something, but perhaps you weren't all that interested in listening to something new? Perhaps you humored someone, listened grudgingly, but then, against your pre-judgments, the music started to seep in? Perhaps, somehow, your response changed. I know I have experienced this many, many times in my life, certainly in my earlier years, when the unknown seemed bothersome, and I preferred to stay in my comfort zone.

There seems to be an age, perhaps around eight to ten years old, when we begin to shut out new things. The wonderment of childhood begins to give way to practical realities. Instead of a youthful thirst for experience, wanting to go *everywhere,* experience *everything,* we start to prefer the stability of our creature comforts. So it is with music, too. When we open ourselves up to truly listen to music we may be unfamiliar with, it gives us a chance to *feel* that music.

"I think of it as getting people to *unfold their*

arms," Ben told me. "Most people approach music with folded arms. You can't get to their heart that way. You have to get them to drop their arms. Because we think we're full. We like to hang on to stuff and feel like we've got it all figured out; we don't have any room for something unfamiliar. But you have to leave yourself open to that connection. You have to leave yourself open to the *vibrations.*"

The more I thought about that openness to vibrations, the more it made sense to me. Perhaps because music had not been readily available in my home growing up, whenever I am introduced to a new style, it often takes me a moment to acclimate—to unfold my arms—and to beat back my initial reactions, which are often akin to those words Johnny Carson mouthed so memorably during my performance on his show in 1968. When I was a father of daughters in the 1960s and rock 'n' roll was making waves, I didn't understand it. My kids were listening to these rock bands, and I thought it was just noise.

How can anyone listen to this? I thought. This had to be an aberration. As much as I didn't know about music, I thought this was an anomaly. I could not understand rock 'n' roll. I wasn't alone in this initial (and, in hindsight, mistaken) assessment of this new musical genre, and its premier performers. An authority no less than James Bond himself declared in 1964's

160

Goldfinger that "there are some things that just aren't done, such as drinking Dom Perignon '53 above the temperature of thirty-eight degrees Fahrenheit." This, he opined, was "as bad as listening to the Beatles without earmuffs." Agent 007 and I were in complete agreement.

Years later, I was asked to perform a rock song. *Oh great,* I thought. But I said yes, as is my wont, and began rehearsing.

And that's when it hit me. As the cacophony surrounded me and I belted out lyrics, for the first time I began to understand what rock 'n' roll was all about. It was music, yes, but it was deeper than loud guitars and drums with complementary words. It was about *energy.* It was about vim and joy and heartache and victory. An explosion of human need, expressed by riling up our most savage spirit and forcing it out into the world with harmonic sound. Then it made sense to me. I started to listen to rock 'n' roll very differently, and I now count Queen as my favorite band and "Bohemian Rhapsody" as my favorite song.

On that note, a quick word: Never be ashamed of the music you love. Even if your father thinks it's just noise. If you have found a sound that appeals to you, if you have opened your heart to let that vibration into your body and soul, then love it. Love it with every fiber of your being. Others don't have to agree with you; your connection to music is your own.

But Bill, you must be thinking, *sometimes music can just be music. It doesn't have to be meaningful on a deeper level.* To you I say, "How many albums have you made?" All kidding aside, that could very well be true for many people; all I can tell you is what music means to me, and how that meaning has evolved over the years.

The same journey I had experienced in coming to understand rock 'n' roll repeated itself when I learned about rap.

I was playing a satirical version of myself in Robert Meyer Burnett and Mark A. Altman's wonderful romantic comedy *Free Enterprise*. In the film's climax, I try to prove my bona fides as a serious entertainer by performing a rap version of Marc Antony's famous soliloquy from *Julius Caesar*. The rap was composed and produced by Rated R (a.k.a. Walter Burns). He was in his early twenties when I met him to work on the song. I went down to his Culver City studio, a large, darkened room filled with marijuana smoke; his entourage of four or five associates sat on a couch near us as Rated R got out his pencil and paper.

"What's this all about?" he asked me. "You know, 'Friends, Romans, countrymen' . . . what is Marc Antony saying here?" I gave him a detailed explanation about how Marc Antony is there to give a speech at Caesar's funeral; he was Caesar's friend, but the conventional wisdom of the crowd was that Caesar was a tyrant, and they were sympathetic to his assassination. Marc Antony saw things very differently, but he had to walk a fine line in indicating his general admiration of the conspirators ("Brutus is an honorable man") while subtly changing the crowd's feelings on the subject, and ultimately bringing them around to turn them against Brutus and Cassius.

Rated R was intrigued by the story. He began to write, riffing on lines from the speech, figuring out how to punctuate them with music, and he created an extraordinary rap called "No Tears for Caesar." Watching his process and hearing the eventual composition, I was floored. "This is the best thing I've ever heard," I told Rated R, to his delight. The song was a memorable part of the film, and my interest in the language and structure of rap took off.

I became fascinated by rap battles, in which artists freestyle lyrics off the top of their heads in competition with each other. I would watch them with my jaw hanging, absolutely astounded that these young people could come up with words that not only rhymed but had incredible wit attached to them, in direct service of the battle with their opposing artist. It is an art form, plain and simple, and one of which I remain in awe every time I hear a new song.

I loved Metallica in the eighties, Nirvana in the nineties, rap in the aughts. Bands and artists who conveyed a sense of attitude, of yearning for something and desirous of an authentic way to express it.

Even to this day, I don't wait in anticipation for an artist's album to "drop" and then immediately download it on my iPhone (or, more accurately, ask my assistant, Kathleen, how to download it on my iPhone, and then just hand her the phone, so she can do it). I listen now much in the way I listened then. I'll hear a song in passing, or on the radio in my car, or someone will say, "Bill, you've gotta hear this song!" And then I find myself listening to that song or artist, trying to understand their process and intentions, just as many listeners have tried to understand mine.

I believe my musical journey has culminated in my latest album, *Bill*, although I have found myself yearning for further expression, and by the time you read this, I expect to be hard at work on another record. Because I've found something. I've found meaning and been given the opportunity to express that meaning.

On *Bill*, I collaborated with some of the giants of the musical world. After all these years, these artists not only *got* what I was trying to do but have helped me realize it in ways I could only dream of back in that studio in the sixties. It was my friend Rob Sharenow who made it happen. Rob and I would meet at our favorite restaurant whenever he was in Los Angeles. We'd eat and talk about everything—family, business, art, philosophy. We were sympatico.

One day, Rob brought a friend of his, Dan Miller. Rob and Dan had met in college, and both were into music; Rob had maintained an interest, whereas Dan had made it the focus of his career, playing guitars and keyboards with They Might Be Giants, among others, and showcasing his incredible skills as a composer in film and television.

"We should do an album together," Dan suggested.

Music to my ears.

We chatted about the possibilities, but it was Rob who pitched the idea we all rallied around: "Let's just make it about Bill's life. He's had such a fascinating life and he's got great stories. We'll turn them into songs, and we'll write great music to accompany his words."

We got to work.

Then the pandemic hit.

And yet, we found a way of working that was impervious to the virus. Since we lived on different coasts anyway, we had mostly been communicating by phone and email. We'd talk about a story from my life and break it down into its narrative elements, finding the logical beginning, middle, and end points of the story. From there, Rob and I would work on lyrics, sending ideas back and forth until we were satisfied. Rob's way with words is unmatched. I am in absolute awe of his command of emotion and imagery. I would give him an idea I was trying to express, and he would deliver poetry that brought tears to my eyes. He is a remarkable artist and a wonderful friend, and without him the album could only have been a shell of what it became. Armed with a completed lyric, we'd hand things over to Dan and he would put the words to music. Other times, we went the other way around: Dan would come up with a rhythmic pattern, and Rob and I would excavate the stories of my life to put words to Dan's music.

As COVID-19 made video chatting ubiquitous, we likewise jumped on Zoom to discuss the music and listen to Dan's compositions. Together, the three of us formed a wonderful artistic bond, always pushing ourselves to make each song the best it could possibly be, and to try to achieve that original concept of putting spoken words to meaningful musical accompaniment.

To my utter delight, other titans of music put their hands up to collaborate with us. Dan had formed a connection with Let's Get It! Records, which was Joe Jonas's label underneath Republic Records and Universal Music. Joe and Dan talked, and suddenly Joe was collaborating with us. Then Joe Walsh. Joe Walsh! My goodness. Dave Koz, Brad Paisley, Robert Randolph, John Lurie, Joan As Police Woman, and of course

Dan Miller, making it all happen. For me, having these legends write and play and sing on this album was the ultimate vindication that there was merit in what I had been trying to do all those years ago. I just had to wait. To keep journeying. To continue my musical path, being open to wherever my journey took me, from coming around to rock 'n' roll, to working with Ben Folds, to discovering rap. The current of the universe kept sweeping me along, until I eventually arrived at this crystallizing moment. These artists had found me, and together we had made music.

The songs on *Bill* chart a journey, from my motorcycle riding (the cacophonous tribute "I Ride"), to the lowest point of my life, when I was broke and divorced, and yet witnessing the highest heights of humanity as man first walked on the moon ("So Far from the Moon"), to the pain and regret of keeping one of my beautiful horses to stud instead of just letting him live his life in freedom ("Black Horse"). Rob Sharenow and I wrote a song about loneliness, aptly called "Loneliness." As I mentioned in an earlier chapter, I had wanted Yo-Yo Ma to play cello on the song, to express the resonance of true solitude. The sonorous essence of emptiness: a sobbing and begging, given form through the timbre of the cello.

Yo-Yo Ma's schedule didn't permit him to

contribute, but that gave way to a new perspective on the subject matter. Instead of the isolation, we thought about the *weight*. The crushing pain of feeling like you have no one. That became the essence of the song, and in Yo-Yo Ma's place we were blessed with John Lurie, who played a haunting saxophone to manifest that crush, that foreboding sense of gravity pulling you down, as you struggle against desolation and emptiness.

It felt so right, I knew in my soul that Yo-Yo Ma's cello was saving itself for a future collaboration.

The album concludes with the cosmic "What Do We Know," which asks those questions I find myself asking every day, and which form the soul of this book, this journey I am on to uncover the bonds that entangle and unite all people and things:

Mindfulness taught me
To try to live life
Aware of each moment
Free of judgment or strife
But lately my thoughts drift beyond
    waking breath
I find time better spent to be pondering
    death
But lately my thoughts
Drift beyond waking breath
I find time better spent

To be pondering death
What do we know?
What are the answers
A baby's birth
A murderous cancer
Why should we care?
What should we do?
Is there something beyond
Just me and you?
Shakespeare, he wrote
Seven ages began
With the sputtering child
To the drooling old man
Yes, the world is a stage
And we all merely play
But as to what's next
Even he couldn't say
What do we know?
What are the answers
A baby's birth
A murderous cancer
Why should we care?
What should we do?
Is there something beyond
Just me and you?
Always worshipped hellos
And avoided goodbyes
Crave the parting of lips
And the spreading of thighs
If it's all an illusion

Fame, power, and wealth
I'll cling to sensation
There may be nothing else
What do we know?
What are the answers
A baby's birth
A murderous cancer
Why should we care?
What should we do?
Is there something beyond
Just me and you?
Yet, the more we discover
The more we unfold
The mysteries deepen
And have greater hold
We're in love with the mystery
What might be out there
Stand shoulder to shoulder
Humbly searching the air
And I tune in the world
Every sound, taste and smell
From the tiniest insects
To the clamorous bells
Everything comes together
Like a deep ocean blue
If life is sensation
Perhaps death is too
What do we know?
What are the answers
A baby's birth

A murderous cancer
Why should we care?
What should we do?
Is there something beyond
Just me and you?

I believe I've got at least one more album in me, but if I had to close the book on my music career, I could not have asked for a better way to go out—with that song and those lyrics. My musical journey has been a beautiful, soul-enriching experience. When all is said and done, isn't that the greatest music of all?

— CHAPTER 6 —

THE WORST AND THE BEST

Ninety-one years is a long time, and while I am confident my race has not yet been fully run, I am painfully aware that I have many more days behind me than in front. More memories to recall than to create. It's easy to say that every success and failure, every right and left turn, brought me to this point in time; *of course they did.* But as I look back, I find there is so much more to celebrate than to mourn, and for those things we do have to grieve over, it's important to never lose sight of the fact that in spite of what we have lost, *we are still here.* That is a gift. Each day we are here brings the promise of another tomorrow, with more to discover and more to experience.

In earlier chapters, I recalled some of the worst moments of my life. In the wake of an unspeakable nightmare, I wasn't sure that I wanted to go on living. In those darkest passages, my family rescued me. In the time since, I have been inspired by the examples of others who have risen like a phoenix out of the ashes of personal tragedy. I have also watched helplessly as some have been unable to reemerge from the darkness of despair and depression.

Robert Ballard was fascinated by the ocean. He studied, among other things, marine geology, and grew obsessed with undersea exploration; he became known as the go-to guy for finding all things underwater. Ballard discovered the *Bismarck* and was able to conclude definitively that while it had sustained damage from British torpedoes during its final battle, it had been, in fact, scuttled by the crew to prevent it from falling into Allied hands. He also located the ocean liner *Lusitania*, sunk in 1915 by a German U-Boat in controversial circumstances.

Ballard is best known, however, for finding the wreck of the *Titanic* in 1985 after failing in an earlier attempt in 1977. The story is Hollywood worthy, not dissimilar from the plot of *Argo*, which involved the cover story of making a film to disguise an effort to rescue American diplomats trapped in Iran. (As it happens, *Argo* was the name of Ballard's robotic deep-sea craft, which played a major role in his discoveries.)

What was unknown to all but a select few at the time was that the entire search for the *Titanic* had been a cover story for a military operation. During Cold War training exercises, the United States had lost two separate nuclear submarines, the USS *Thresher* and USS *Scorpion*, but did not have the technology and expertise necessary to do close-up surveillance of the wrecks. This left the Navy concerned about the possibility of the wrecks being pillaged by the Soviet Union, and the potential of radioactivity from the nuclear reactors in the subs harming the environment.

The Navy struck a deal to allow Ballard to search for the *Titanic* after he'd first surveyed the *Thresher* and *Scorpion*. A giant media frenzy ensued, disguising the true nature of the mission, and Ballard was able to use the Navy's funds and resources to find the long-lost ship of dreams.

From the absolute highs of his professional life, Ballard was then struck with utter tragedy. In 1989, just weeks after his discovery of the *Bismarck*, his son Todd, who had accompanied and assisted him in the expedition, took a corner too fast in his father's old T-Bird, and slammed into a tree. He and his friend were killed instantly. Todd was just twenty years old.

Ballard fell into a deep, crushing depression. It is often said that tragedy can bring people closer together, as they take stock of what they have lost and vow to hold on to what they still have, but it is also often the case that when two parents lose a *child,* it becomes impossible for them to keep their marriage alive. When the very sight of your partner reminds you of the worst loss imaginable, it can become unbearable to even look at them. And so it was with Robert and Marjorie, his wife of twenty-four years. Their marriage had been strained for some time, but it was damaged beyond repair by the sudden loss of their son, and they divorced a year later.

Ballard was shattered, but over time he recovered, finding an inner strength and rededicating himself to his work, his children, and his family.

I understand some of the grief that Robert Ballard experienced. While I cannot even conceive the unfathomable pain of losing a child, as you know, I lost my wife Nerine in 1999. One of the most unbearable aspects of this agonizing loss was the feeling that Nerine had, in a way, taken her own life. She was not suicidal, and yet her addiction to alcohol was a version of a slow-simmering suicide. Though she died in an accident, it was years of self-harm through addiction that allowed that awful set of circumstances to eventuate.

As I was preparing to marry Nerine, my dear friend Leonard Nimoy, himself recovering from alcoholism, sat me down and told me that she was a fellow addict. If I was going to marry her, it was something I would have to be prepared to deal with, to try to understand, he counseled. Oh, I was so naive. I thought that my love for Nerine could "cure" her, but in hindsight, that was like hoping love could cure a broken leg or a brain tumor. Illness simply doesn't work that way.

While love could not cure Nerine's addiction, neither could logic. She knew intellectually that she was drinking herself into an early grave. On more than one occasion, I asked her, pleadingly, "Don't you want to live?"

"Yes, I want to live," she would reply, then proceed to drink herself into another tragic alcohol poisoning so harmful that it would require drying out at a hospital. Perhaps, toward the end, Nerine knew that if she drank enough, she could end her addiction at the cost of her life, and perhaps that played a part in her actions. I can only speculate. Much like I didn't understand addiction, I have always had difficulty understanding suicide and depression. While I have felt some of the deepest sorrow one can feel and, in those moments, contemplated the idea that perhaps I didn't want to live anymore, I have been blessed with never having had to battle the actual sickness of depression.

How does one get to a point in which they say to themselves, "I can't take it anymore"? When is there too much pain to justify continuing to live?

Anthony Bourdain is someone I have thought about a lot when pondering the tragedy of suicide. His life as a chef was a celebration of something so foundational to human existence; his joy of making food is a metaphor for life itself. Here was this incredible man whose vocational and spiritual purpose was to nourish humanity with food and its plentiful stories, exploring all manner of cultures and culinary influences to make that food taste better.

But underneath it all, Bourdain was traveling with the cruel passenger that is depression. While our attitudes toward mental health are slowly changing for the better, it is still a deadly ailment that many suffer from in silence, lest others think less of them. Indeed, many sufferers have found the courage to confide in a loved one about their condition, only to be told, "Everyone feels sad sometimes," or "Cheer up and look on the bright side of life," as if wishing it is enough to make it so. Sadly, these well-meaning platitudes can do more damage, as they tend to minimize the very real feelings of the sufferer. If you're depressed and someone tries to remind you how much worse your life could be, that is likely to cause guilt, not alleviate your pain.

There is no amount of material or even spiritual wealth that can turn around depression in and of itself. Bourdain was not short on either. He was a vigorous man, traveling to all corners of the globe and experiencing a great deal of joy wherever he went. But between those moments of happiness, there was loneliness. I have experienced it myself: I might travel to a convention or appearance somewhere, and while I am surrounded by love at the event itself, the bookends of that experience are longer by far than the experience itself. There is a trip on an airplane, which I usually take alone; there is time before the event and after, in which I am alone in a hotel room or eating alone at a restaurant. In that time, I don't have any meaningful interactions; I don't talk to anyone. Because he was suffering from depression, those moments alone for Anthony Bourdain must have been profoundly difficult to endure.

As I write these words, I realize that I am attempting to rationalize what happened to Anthony Bourdain, trying to apply logic to a condition that defies logic. Like addiction, depression is difficult to tame. There is no "cure" as such, but there are psychological and psychiatric treatments; there are methods to cope. In battling the deepest, darkest recesses of the mind, humanity has shown an incredible ability to adapt.

Adaptation, in the simplest terms, is our ability to *bend* in order to cope with challenges, be they physical, psychological, or otherwise. If you don't bend with the circumstances of your life, it can break you. But if you find a way to bend, you can get through nearly any challenge you face. If you're fighting a current, you can go with the flow while attempting to catch a branch to pull yourself out.

I know someone who had attempted suicide (unsuccessfully, thankfully) in their seventies. That would seem, on the surface, a very unusual age at which to decide one can't go on living any longer. This person was not living with a painful disease, or the threat of one, such as happened to Robin Williams when he was diagnosed with Lewy body dementia, which he knew would eventually torture and hijack both his mind and body.

I asked this person who had attempted suicide what was going through his mind in the lead-up to this decision to end it all. He told me that in that moment, the sadness he felt was so strong and he had no sense of how he might make himself feel better. Suicide seemed like the only viable option.

As luck would have it, and without being too indelicate in my description, the method with which he chose to end his life was momentarily reversible, and he was able to grab that meta-phorical branch and stop himself from ultimately going through with it. Heartbreakingly, Anthony Bourdain, and in a different way, Nerine, were unable to free themselves from the forces pulling them down.

Of course, it is true that one need not suffer from clinical depression to *be depressed* or find themselves enduring such pain that they wonder whether they can go on.

I suffer from a hearing condition called tinnitus, a constant ringing or hissing in the ears. It can be confounding, not just because of the unrelenting irritation, but because despite how loud it is to the sufferer, no one else around them can hear it. *It's all in your head,* as they say (except it actually is!); no matter how close I put my ear to someone else's, they cannot hear it, and I look very silly for going through the exercise. I most likely developed the condition on the set of *Star Trek* when Leonard Nimoy and I were both standing too close to an explosion that went off as part of a special effect. Leonard suffered from the condition as well.

The most difficult part of tinnitus is that it never stops. It is unwavering. It doesn't take a break, and sadly, for some that can be too much. I have known fellow sufferers who have ended their own lives rather than go on with that noise inside their heads. The thought had occurred to me in my early years, but after much practice, concentration, and meditation, I eventually learned to live with it and tune it out.

I have tried to pass on what I have learned to others who struggle with tinnitus, although since I am not inside their heads, it is impossible for me to know exactly what they are dealing with. I can only hope that my lived experience, empathy, and coping strategies can be useful to them. I became friendly with a great jazz musician who had become afflicted by it. This is common among musicians, who are accustomed to playing next to gargantuan speaker systems.

"Bill," he told me, "I can't live with this. I don't know if I can go on."

"You *can* go on," I exhorted. Over the course of several conversations, I slowly talked him down and shared with him my coping techniques.

An Oscar-winning actor who also suffers from tinnitus heard through the grapevine that I had some mechanisms for how to defeat—or at least live with—this ailment. I was immediately empathetic, but on a different level. I knew what he was going to say before he said it. "I can't learn my lines."

I relayed to him the story of a country boy moving to the city. Where once he had slept to the quiet, peaceful whistle of the country-side wind, he found himself awakened nonstop by the sounds of heavy footfalls, garbage cans, and honking cars. Six months later, it became background noise; without realizing it, the tumult had all melded into harmless ambient sound.

"You will become habituated," I reassured the actor. A doctor once told me that fear multiplies itself. You are afraid of something, and then you become aware that you are afraid, which makes you even more afraid. "It is the same with tinnitus," I said. "Once you get over the initial fear and realize that there are methods to help, you slowly become acclimated."

I believe it is the same with personal grief. When you lose someone or something you care about, the grief and fear take hold of you. You feel that you cannot go on without what you've just lost.

David Kessler is one of the world's foremost experts on grief. He was an associate of the late psychiatrist and author Elisabeth Kübler-Ross, who was best known for developing what is commonly known as the "five stages of grief," articulated in her groundbreaking international bestseller *On Death and Dying*. Kessler cowrote *On Grief and Grieving* with Kübler-Ross, which was published shortly before her death, and he has since taken up her sword in the all-important work of educating the world on how we deal with grief and death. I was fortunate enough to meet and interview Kessler for my show *I Don't Understand*.

Kessler explained to me that the immediate impact of death causes grief that is at its strongest for around a year. As you navigate the stages of grief, you eventually arrive at acceptance, and from there, your life can begin again. That is not to say you will not still be grieving, or that everything will be back to normal; it means you will have been sufficiently freed from the heaviest chains of grief so that you can look forward with some sort of inspiration, and ideally, a hope that your life will continue and that you will learn something from your grieving. It is as painful as anything you could do to your body, but human beings have incredible mental resilience, and you will eventually habituate to your new circumstances.

That hit very close to home for me. I know that I have learned from the grief in my life. At ninety-one years old, each day can bring with it the painful news of a lost friend or the end of a chapter. I am better equipped now to deal with such pain, and even though there is great sadness involved, I can choose to remember the best of times and look to the next day for an opportunity for more.

Of course, I can only speak from my own experience. Maybe this river of fate I'm floating on is just big enough for one, a kayak measured solely for me. We each deal with loss in our own way. Sometimes, the best way to look at pain is to laugh at it. For me, having been performing since the age of six, I have thought about the worst and the best in my career. As an actor, you live in fear of those moments. Are you acting in an absolute turkey of a film? Is the play you're doing going to flop?

The worst experience of my professional career began in triumph and then took a very strange turn. In the late seventies, I was asked to perform a reading of some great works of science fiction literature, accompanied by an orchestra playing pieces by the great Russian composer Igor Stravinsky. The performance was in Anaheim

Stadium, around thirty miles outside of Los Angeles.

The night was warm. An electrical storm played nearby, dazzling the outdoor audience with its intermittent flashes. A crowd of thirty thousand sat before me and yet they maintained such a blessed silence that even my whispers could be heard clearly. If someone had yelled out, "Captain Kirk!" or "We love you, Bill!" (or, heaven forbid, something less positive), it might have destroyed everything. But the crowd held their peace in rapt attention, and rose to their feet in thunderous applause at the conclusion. It was a magical, perfect moment.

Years later, in a similar vein, I was invited to perform some poetry as part of an evening of classical music and pieces by the great composer John Williams. It was a treat to be on that bill. The concept for my part of the show was to blend poetry and classical accompaniment and all manner of sounds that complemented the words I would speak. Our first performance was at the Hollywood Bowl. I stepped out onto the stage, the phenomenal Los Angeles Philharmonic orchestra behind me, and began my first piece, D. H. Lawrence's "Whales Weep Not!"

They say the sea is cold, but the sea contains the hottest blood of all, and the wildest, the most urgent.

The orchestra glided over the words, and underneath, *whale song,* sounds of marine life, punctuated my recitation. Just like at the Stravinsky performance years earlier at Anaheim Stadium, the crowd at the Hollywood Bowl gave me their devotion as I read these powerful words, the orchestra pushing me on, the soundscapes echoing perfectly from the speakers. It was wonderful. It was rapturous.

Then came Vancouver.

Oh, Vancouver.

I should have known something was wrong. Moments before I was due to make my entrance, I sneaked a peek from the wings out into the crowd. I saw a whole bunch of guys in black leather motorcycle jackets, tending vigorously to their beers. It was a smaller, much more intimate venue than Anaheim Stadium or the Hollywood Bowl, and I guess people don't really get too dressed up for the symphony anymore, but this didn't look right. Then again, I justified to myself, I hadn't lived in Canada for a couple of decades, and I'd always been an East Coast boy, so perhaps this is just how they did things in British Columbia.

The PA boomed and it was time to go. "Ladies and gentlemen, please welcome William Shatner!"

It started off well. I got great cheers. Shame on me for being so closed-minded. It was a reminder to never judge a book by its cover. These bikers must have been more cultured than I gave them credit for, as they were *Star Trek* fans. They were also able to swill pints while admiring classical music, and even better, poetry and whale sounds. An impressive crowd, these West Coast Canucks!

The orchestra started. The soundscapes didn't. No ocean sounds, no whale songs.

Looking to the wings, I was greeted with a shrug from the stage manager. *Okay,* I thought, *I'll figure it out. I've got this.*

Now, I don't mean to say that the words of D. H. Lawrence without an orchestra aren't entertaining in and of themselves; of course they are. But there was something lost without the intertwined ocean sounds that had been so successful in the previous performances.

I continued with the poetry, trying to invigorate with my performance what had been left behind by the failure of the sound effects to play. The crowd was silent, but not in rapt awe. They were confused. Drunk and confused.

"Boo!" I heard.

I ignored it. D. H. Lawrence isn't everybody's cup of tea, I told myself.

Then another boo rang out. Then another. I was drowning. What was going on?

"Get off the stage!" a man bellowed.

It continued. I finished my poem and got off the stage.

"What the hell is going on?" I asked whomever I could get my hands on.

It turned out that there had been a mistake with the scheduling and advertising of the venue. These bikers were here for a metal concert. The last thing they were expecting was me and an orchestra and whale poetry (without whale sounds!).

I don't know why it had taken them this long to figure it all out. There was an orchestra on the stage, for crying out loud! Maybe they thought they were going to get a juxtaposition of heavy metal against classical backing, like when Metallica played with the San Francisco Symphony.

The experience in Vancouver was so shocking that for a few moments we considered stopping the tour, but when we took in all the information and realized the profound misunderstanding that had led to this humiliation onstage, we soldiered on. The next date was in Seattle, and it was a return to the well-received performances we had delivered in California. Truthfully, I kept a brave face plastered on for the rest of the tour; I was terrified each time I stepped out onstage. Fear can be a powerful motivator for an actor, but this was more akin to severe anxiety, and I was grateful when the tour ended.

There have been episodes of my life in which the binary nature of an audience's response has taken a back seat to larger issues and woken up a part of my social conscience.

In 1962, Roger Corman directed me in *The Intruder*, written by *Twilight Zone* writer Charles Beaumont, based on his 1959 novel of the same name. The film is about forced desegregation in the South. I played a particularly odious character by the name of Adam Cramer, who tries to rile up the local townsfolk to fight back against federally ordered integration, and against Black people specifically. The film received decent reviews but was a failure at the box office.

The film's disappointing receipts were painful, but what I remember vividly about *The Intruder* is that as Hollywood filmmakers, we were *not* welcome in East Prairie, Missouri, where the film was made. Crew were harassed, equipment was broken, the locals called us Communists. We weren't sure how safe we were. The actors were being lodged in a local motel, and I literally had an escape route memorized that would have taken me out of the bathroom window and into a nearby cornfield.

While Missouri was not technically a Southern state (though it stood in for one in the film), integration was a relatively new concept and there was a lot of backlash. The idea of a bunch of Hollywood folks coming in to shoot a preachy film about it rubbed a lot of people the wrong way.

Here we were, shooting a film about rabble-rousing in an area that was already prone to rabble-rousing. Toward the end of the shoot, we had to film a scene in which my character goes on a terribly racist rant in front of the townspeople. An ad had gone out on local radio inviting folks down to where we were shooting if they wanted to be extras in the film. A great number of them showed up, but I had gotten rather hoarse from the previous day's shooting, so my voice was almost completely gone.

Roger Corman came to me and said, "I'll shoot over your shoulder first, so we'll get all the crowd reactions." To save my voice, I mimed the speech and all the actions; Corman would then tell the audience how to react—yell, shout, wave your hands, etc. Of course, as anyone who has visited a film set can tell you, moviemaking is not always all that exciting. There's a lot of waiting around. The scene had started around eight or nine in the evening, and as we kept shooting, the crowd started to disperse. By midnight, most of them had gone home. By then, I had regained just enough of my voice to make a decent showing of the speech for my close-ups. We did them and then wrapped for the night.

The next day, Roger and I were walking down one of the main streets of East Prairie. The publisher of the local newspaper saw us and flagged us down. He had been there when we shot the scene the night before.

"You guys are very smart," he said. Roger and I looked at each other quizzically.

"Why do you say that?" Roger asked.

The publisher pointed at me. "Because he didn't say anything. During that crowd scene, you filmed the crowd and he didn't say anything until they were all gone."

"Yeah," Roger replied, "that's how it's usually done. We film one side just for the reactions, then we turn the camera around to get the speech."

"You don't understand," the publisher explained. "There's a tree near where you were filming. Twenty years ago, people in this town lynched a Black man from that tree. There were people working for you as extras last night who were part of that hanging. If they had heard what you said in your close-up, there's no telling what would have happened."

I felt so naive. I had thought we were just making a movie. It was on a charged subject, yes, but I couldn't appreciate the enormity of it. Moreover, filming *The Intruder* made me very aware of how much I didn't understand about race relations. I can't fathom what is in the hearts of people who persecute others merely for the color of their skin. More terrifyingly, I cannot imagine what it is like to be Black in a place like that.

I was a Jewish boy growing up in a part of Montreal where the other kids were all too keen to bully me for being Jewish, but if you see me in the street, you don't know immediately that I'm Jewish. It is why white Jews like me have, to a degree, been able to pass free from surface prejudice. We don't know what it is like to be Black, to live under the constant threat of humiliation, or worse. Regardless of whether *The Intruder* turned out to be successful, I gained a valuable perspective on the true nature of race relations in America. It was an ugly time in Missouri in 1962, and sadly, it remains ugly to this day.

Years later, in 1974, I had another (much less fraught) opportunity to work with Roger Corman when he produced *Big Bad Mama*, a pseudo follow-up to 1970's *Bloody Mama*, which he'd directed. The film became an unexpected cult hit, but what I look back on fondly was my time working with Angie Dickinson. Oh, she was lovely. I think I fell a little in love with her.

Angie and I had to do a sex scene, and I remember she seemed quite nervous about it. We had started the production with a table read and discussion at Roger's house, and he confirmed that she and I would need to be nude for the scene. Angie was apprehensive; she'd never done a nude scene before and wanted Roger's assurance that only the most essential folks would be present on set. Roger gave her that assurance. I had no particular desire to be naked for hours on end in front of any more people than necessary, so I agreed: the set should be closed during the nude scene.

We started shooting the film; a couple of weeks later, it was time for the scene. We each disrobed and got into the bed. Lighting was set, camera was set, makeup was set. The director cleared almost everyone out. Angie and I were undressed, ready to roll.

"Wait a second," Angie said. "We can't do the scene without the makeup artist. What if he needs to adjust my makeup? Come on, Alan, you'd better stay."

Okay, so Alan the makeup artist needed to stay. Now time for the scene.

"Hang on," Angie said. "We can't do the scene without my hair stylist. What if he needs to adjust my hair? Gene, Gene! Come back!"

So, Gene the hair stylist returned to set. Now we can shoot the scene. *Did I mention I'm lying here naked?!*

But Angie wasn't done. One by one, she invited every crew member back to the set. Can't do the scene without the sound mixer; we can't proceed without the grip and electrical guys; come on, we can't shoot the scene without the entire art department here . . .

The crew all applauded as Angie invited each department member and their dog back to the "closed" set. To this day, I don't know if she was playing with me. But I enjoyed every minute I spent in her delightful company.

When I think about the ups and downs of my career, the greatest highlight would have to be putting together my one-man show, *Shatner's World: We Just Live in It* at the Music Box Theatre on Broadway in 2012. We took the title and many of the stories from a book I wrote with the hilarious Chris Regan called *Shatner Rules*. The show was conceived as a ninety-minute piece of entertainment in which I would take the audience through the highlights (and lowlights) of my career, regaling them with stories of show business, family, and up till then, my eighty-something years of life.

For actors, a performance is always, at least on some level, frightening. You are putting yourself out there for the world to see, inviting them into your process and displaying what you hope is your best work, in the interest of getting a pleasing reaction. If you're doing comedy, you want to get the best laughs you can; if you're doing drama, it's your goal to evoke meaningful emotional responses. (If they're laughing when you're doing something dramatic, you've either screwed up or you've presented *The Transformed Man* thirty years ahead of its time!)

If I perform in a film or an episode of television, I'm sheltered from the audience because I don't have to read reviews, and I'm sheltered from self-criticism because I don't have to watch myself. Being onstage, however, is like performing in the bedroom: the feedback is instant. If your work is good, you'll hear the enthusiastic praise; if it's not, you can be greeted by a deafening silence—and that can be truly shattering to your ego and sense of self-worth.

The first performance of *Shatner's World* was an experience the likes of which I had never before encountered. Earlier in the day, I had woken up in all sorts of, shall we say, *gastrointestinal distress*. I was losing fluids and worse from every part of my body and was barely even able to imbibe water. Somehow, by the evening, I was able to pull myself together enough to physically get to the theater, but I was not entirely sure I'd be able to go onstage. This was opening night. It was a packed house. The critics were waiting to write their reviews. What was I supposed to do?

Around this time in my life, I had started to take a philosophical view of hardship—pain, career and familial difficulties, personal struggles. I had tried to give such challenges a *historical* point of view; that is, instead of living in the present with this burden, I tried to imagine what it would be like to look back on it six months or a year into the future. That attitude strengthened my resolve. *Whatever happens to me tonight,* I thought, *will be a hell of a story when I remember it a year from now.*

Boldly, I took my place on the stage and attacked the material with panache. The response was terrific; the audience was eating it up.

Then, about halfway through the show, disaster struck. In my pants.

"Hold up," I told the audience. "We seem to have a small technical difficulty. Please bear with us; I'll be right back."

I raced off the stage and up the stairs to my dressing room. A quick shower and change of underwear later, and I was back in front of the audience. I was not going to be defeated by defecation in my Dockers!

The rest of the show went without incident. To my great satisfaction, the reviews (which were great) didn't even mention the "technical difficulty" that had paused the show for ten minutes. I performed *Shatner's World* on Broadway for just under a month before taking the show on a national and later international tour.

To stand up and hold an audience captive for ninety minutes and have them cheer at the end . . . that was the pinnacle of my career—because it was something that I was able to achieve truly without artifice. There were no other performers to cover for me if I wasn't pulling my weight; there were no special effects or dancing ladies to provide misdirection. *Shatner's World* proved to me that I was enough. More than enough, I was capable.

To me, all the accolades and awards and critical praise in the world cannot compare to the gratification of pleasing an audience all by myself. It was also the biggest risk I had ever taken in my career. To be onstage like that, truly alone, is to be at your most vulnerable, your most exposed. As they say, you can die from *exposure.*

I believe that virtually every performance of *Shatner's World* ended in a standing ovation. I recall being on the stage, taking in that energy, and thinking to myself, *Wow. I did that.* If I were so inclined, perhaps I could have hung up my hat after that run. But if you've learned anything about me in these pages, you'll know that I am relentlessly curious for what's next, for what strange new worlds still might be out there for me to explore.

And so, as always, I venture forth. Into the unknown.

— CHAPTER 7 —

THERE'S BEAUTY IN EVERYTHING

There's a lesser-known Dr. Seuss book published in 1973 called *Did I Ever Tell You How Lucky You Are?* A wise man, somehow sitting benignly on top of a cactus, sings to a young child, telling tales of some of the more wretched circumstances that others are going through. The stories are told in rhyming verse and are filled with the usual Seussian wordplay, onomatopoeia, and incurable optimism. We hear the tale of Mr. Bix, who has a "borfin" to fix; poor Harry Haddow, who "can't make any shadow." It's a cute book and illustrative of a central point: we are so blessed to be alive, to be living and thriving; whatever our circumstances are, they could be so much worse.

To take that a step further, we are lucky to exist at all. To have made it this far as a species is already a miracle, but for every one of us to have even been born is something of a mathematical impossibility.

Dr. Ali Binazir studied at Harvard, UC San Diego, and Cambridge University. He is an author, a personal growth consultant, and a self-described Happiness Engineer. In 2011, he illustrated in a much-circulated infographic the outrageously low odds of each one of us even coming into existence. It began with the probability of your parents ever meeting: one in twenty thousand. Then he added the odds of this couple staying together long enough to have children: an additional one in two thousand. So now you were up to a one-in-forty-million chance of being born.

Then Dr. Binazir took us into the astronomical numbers of sperm and eggs that, when combined, could have resulted in anyone, but wound up being you. A fertile woman will enter childbearing age with around one hundred thousand viable eggs; a man will produce some four trillion sperm during that same period. The odds of that one sperm fertilizing that one egg are 1:400,000,000,000,000,000—that's one in four hundred quadrillion.

Of course, to get to this point, your ancestors all had to be born and live and reproduce on and on through the ages. There were several more calculations, and eventually Dr. Binazir suggested we think of the odds like this: "It is the probability of two million people getting together (about the population of San Diego) to play a game of dice with trillion-sided dice. They each roll the dice, and they all come up with the exact same number—for example, 550,343,279,001.

So, the odds that *you* exist at all are *basically zero*."

The infographic closes with these inspiring words: "A miracle is an event so unlikely as to be almost impossible. By that definition, we have just shown that you are a miracle. Now go forth and feel and act like the miracle that you are."

I tell you, I have tears in my eyes reading that. We are miracles. Each and every one of us. And even more than that, the world is a miracle; each particle within it is a miracle.

I was driving through North Hollywood recently on my way to an appointment. I paused at a stop sign and was suddenly distracted by the curvature of a tree. There was no one behind me; I must have stared at that thing for five minutes. It was just a tree, but it got my brain turning. What did it look like before these buildings cropped up around it? What did all of this look like two hundred years ago? What roots had thrived under the surface, connecting this tree to its mother tree, giving it the nutrients it needed to thrust ever upward in search of the sun? Another time, I was in my backyard and happened upon two snails; they were quivering in delight, or what I presume was delight, as they were mating. It may sound silly on the surface, but we're talking about the continuation of life, of creation. And it is all around us.

Everything in the universe has a structure.

Whether it's alive or not, it has a structure and an evolution. In ages past, there was basalt rock, standing there firm and black and solid. After, it became sand and dirt. The evolution of life in every form has such beauty in it. Discovered in 1953 by Watson and Crick, the double helix—hidden from us unless we view it under a powerful microscope—is gorgeous in its simplicity. Two strands perfectly wrapped around each other in harmony.

Everything renews; change is constant and all around us.

As Blue Origin took me to space, I was pulverized with feelings of sadness, because when I looked down and saw our fragile blue planet, all I could think of was the damage that humankind perpetrates daily. Looking out into space, sadly, did not fill me with the optimism Gene Roddenberry had espoused all those years ago; if anything, it made me even more determined that we must explore the beauty of our own world before we ever think about seeking out new ones and their civilizations. What we know here on Earth is beautiful; what we don't know is even more beautiful because it is still there for us to discover. The acquisition of knowledge is beauty and love combined.

To lose your sense of wonder about all of that is to lose your sense of the mystery of life. My dear reader, I hope you leave yourself open to looking at the bewilderment of riches that abound our very senses. Through discovery and then machinery, we have amplified these riches and gained more knowledge, and it is staggering. The beauty that's out there, that's in here, that's all around us. Whether you're talking about a molecule or a grouping of stars, it is all around us. Where there isn't an answer, there's a question—and questions can be even more tantalizing than answers, because they give us mystery; they give us wonder. They give us a chance to discover discovery itself.

I am fortunate that in my life I have been exposed to a great deal of nature and been able to see that beauty up close, privately in my travels as well as publicly on television in several episodes of *The American Sportsman*. The show was a lifestyle series that ran on ABC from 1965 to 1986 and involved taking celebrities out into nature for recreational activities. There were three adventures that stand out to me for their demonstrations of the beauty of the natural world. Two fill me with joy to recollect; the other fills me with dread and regret.

"We're gonna take you white-water kayaking!" a producer announced to me. It was 1972 and they were prepping my upcoming episode. "What do you think?"

"I'll try anything once," I responded. Shortly thereafter, we were off to the Salmon in Idaho, also known, they tell me ominously, as "The River of No Return." My confidence took a slight hit.

I'd never been on a kayak, but the show-runners brought a couple of Olympic champion kayakers to teach me. In my earlier years, I was a competent skier; in some ways, the coaches told me, kayaking is not unlike skiing. When you ski, you've got to be loose in the hips because you're going to go over bumps and you need to move flexibly with those bumps; if you're too rigid, you're going to fall on the slopes. Kayaking is similar in that you need to be loose and go with the flow, they explained, but if you fall, you don't hit the snow; you capsize! And when you capsize in a kayak, you go upside down, still in the kayak, held in by a watertight neoprene apron called a "spray skirt." You can't just swim away.

That confidence of mine took another hit.

"Don't worry," the coaches assured me, "you just have to execute what they call an 'Eskimo Roll.' " (Today it is sometimes referred to simply as a "kayak roll.") Essentially, you use the momentum of going under the water to flip your-self upright. I watched them demonstrate, and it was quite remarkable. In just as much time as it took to capsize, they were back up above water once again. That's what comes from having a lot of kayaking experience.

Ah, experience. I didn't have any of that. Okay,

great. The confidence was getting shakier by the minute. But I let none of that show. This was *The American Sportsman*. A show about adventure. About looking nature in the face and saying, "Take me with you on this journey and I will follow you every step of the way."

I was an eager learner, and by the end of the first day, I had developed enough competence in executing the kayak roll that they were prepared to send me out on the rapids. On day two, they took me out to some gentle rapids and had me work on my maneuvering. It went pretty well, my confidence building with each session. What I didn't know was that there was a five-day schedule, and each day, they were building me up to more difficult rapids, which they were planning to film for the program.

Rapids are marked Class I through VI (for professionals only) in order of difficulty. They had started me on a Class I, but as each session and day progressed, they took me to more difficult waters. One, two, three, four. They were attempting to build up my skills for a Class V rapid. What they didn't tell me, or more accurately *show* me, was just how fast the Class V rapids were. In fact, they kept them from me. Each night when we were done, they would drive me in a somewhat circuitous route back to the motel, deliberately hiding the Class V rapids from me.

Day five arrived and the cameras were positioned. They brought me out to the Class V rapid. I stared into it. It was unlike anything I'd practiced on, even though it was only one degree of difficulty from the ones I'd trained on just the day before.

A rapid develops when the bottom of the river undulates or has rocks and logs trapping the flow of the water, which forces the river violently over those obstructions. The force of that water can be quite severe, and if you're not careful, you can find yourself trapped in the undertow.

Sure enough, I found myself caught and lost control of my kayak. It capsized but instead of being able to kayak roll, I found myself lodged, my shoulder pushed up against a sheer rock. I couldn't get my paddle up, couldn't push myself out against the pressure of the water. The Olympic experts had trained me to bail out in a situation like this: I grabbed hold of the spray skirt and pushed it open, which immediately dislodged me from the watertight seal holding me in. I was out of the kayak. It floated to the surface about a dozen feet above me, but the pressure of the water was keeping me under it. Now I was going downstream, underwater, exposed to the sharp, jagged rocks all around me. I distinctly remember looking up and seeing that the kayak was traveling at the same speed I was.

The show had safety kayakers ready to take

action, and as I made my way back to the surface, they grabbed me and pulled me to the shore. "Are you okay?" they asked. "Okay?" I responded, out of breath. "No! I'm not okay. I capsized."

They nodded, appreciating the danger I'd just faced. But they didn't get it. I wasn't upset that I came close to drowning; I was furious that I'd ruined the shot. That could not be the end of my white-water rafting adventure on *The American Sportsman*.

"Let's do it again!" I exclaimed. There was some debate, but I got my way and went back for another run at it. I'm proud to say that on the second take, I nailed it.

Running the rapids was exhilarating, and it made me appreciate even more the beauty and danger of Mother Nature. We think we can tame nature, but we are very much mistaken. We are merely guests on this beautiful, perilous planet. The waters of Earth have created continents, moved mountains, and taken more lives than we can imagine. I was just a passenger—a lucky one at that.

Having traveled with the flow of the water, I set my sights higher up. I wanted to fly.

Well, perhaps it wasn't so A-to-B as that makes it sound. The truth is, I already knew how to fly. I had learned earlier in my life and had mostly flown Cessna light planes, which are like airplanes with tricycle legs.

Many years after my trip down the Salmon River rapids, *The American Sportsman* once again approached me about an adventure. Since I had some flying experience, they wanted to see if I could take my flying to the next level and try some aerobatics.

I was taken down to Florida and driven to Homestead Air Force Base. I looked up into the sky, where a Pitts Special S1 biplane pilot was doing some unbelievable maneuvers. "That guy's incredible!" I remarked to the producer.

"He should be," came the reply. "He's your instructor."

I watched in awe as this fellow—an Air Force flying instructor—completed his maneuvers before eventually coming down with a perfect landing. He disembarked and we were introduced.

"That looping maneuver I saw you do . . . what on earth was that?" I inquired, eagerly.

"That's called a Lomcovák," he replied. "And that's what you're gonna learn. With absolute military precision."

Holy shit. Now here was a challenge.

It's hard to describe in writing, but the Lomcovák is a hell of a maneuver. In the simplest of terms, it involves piloting the aircraft in loops that go tail over front and wing over wing at the same time. It's like doing forward somersaults and barrel rolls simultaneously: a fantastic gyroscopic maneuver in the air. You have to see it to believe it—and even then, it's hard to believe. The instructor took me up and the instant we were in the air, he started the Lomcovák. I was tossed every which way in the air as the aircraft tumbled tail over front and wing over wing. Later, the instructor removed the lid from his cup of coffee and executed a series of loops. The coffee never moved and never spilled. That's how much of an expert he was, and that's the kind of skill he wanted me to have when it came time to shoot the episode.

I spent six days learning basic aerobatic maneuvers in the S-2B two-seater version of the Pitts Special, the instructor at my side as I drilled loops, turns, and Dutch rolls over and over and over again. This guy wasn't kidding around when he said I'd be learning "absolute military precision." He shouted instructions at me like he was a drill sergeant and I was a misbehaving cadet. He was a real grizzled, no-nonsense kind of character.

I took to flying the Pitts Special quickly and enthusiastically. The most difficult thing was landing that sucker. When I'd flown Cessnas, I had three wheels—two primaries and a secondary in front of them. You could look through the windshield of the airplane and see the runway. As you approached the runway, you'd flare the airplane to lose some airspeed, and could glide in for a landing. Not so with the Pitts Special.

On the Pitts Special, there are still three wheels, but it's a taildragger, so the third wheel is way in the back. When you bring it in for a landing, you have to keep the nose of the plane pointed higher in order to bleed off speed, so you're looking at the sky and you can't see the runway through the windshield. Your best bet is to look over the side of the airplane to see if you're over the runway and then judge how to make your landing. Even after you hit the ground, you need to keep pulling back the throttle. You can tail drag right up until you've slowed down to a crawl, so if you're not careful, the plane can wind up doing what they call a "ground loop," which is when the tail of the aircraft loses directional stability and flips back over front—every pilot's worst nightmare (short of death, I suppose). When it comes to landing a taildragger successfully, a pilot relies on their years of experience to get a feel for it.

Oh yes, years of experience. Didn't have those.

I was able to stick the landing supervised and with my instructor barking wind corrections and stabilization methods at me. But on the seventh day, I was supposed to fly solo. On camera.

"Is he ready?" the producer asked. I wished I hadn't been in earshot to hear the instructor's response.

"I don't know . . ."

To hell with it, I decided. I was here, I'd practiced, I was going to do it.

They had decided to try to capture my solo expedition at sunset, known in the film industry as "golden hour." This is a time of day in which the sun is at its lowest and you can capture beautiful, idyllic images with warm natural light. It occurs in the morning within about an hour after sunrise and in the evening starting around an hour before sunset. Truly, it is a magical look on film. That's how I convinced myself that it was a good idea—but if I had thought about it more, I'd have realized that to land a taildragger solo, I'd want as much sunlight as possible!

I had consulted with my family before doing this episode of the show, but as is par for the course, if anything, I was just informing them. We never put anything to a vote; if we had, they were (and still are) so protective of me that I don't think I'd have made it out of the house very often. I certainly never would have made it to space! Somehow, though, as afraid as I could be in the moment, I never thought any harm could befall me. The stunt guys were the ones who got injured; I was just an actor, and all the actors do is make-believe. They don't get hurt because the situations they're in aren't real.

And yet, my situations *were* real. I just never got hurt, never thought I could.

That's the mindset I had going up in that aircraft alone. Danger was my middle name, but death and injury weren't in my vocabulary.

I took the Pitts Special up just before sunset. I executed some great rolls, loops, and maneuvers, all the while being captured on film by two cameras on a follow-plane and several cameras on the ground. The film crew radioed to let me know they'd gotten all the aerobatic footage they needed; now it was time to land. "The lighting is perfect!" they said. They weren't wrong. I gazed out at the horizon, and I was in awe of the majesty of it. The light kissed the tops of distant mountains, clouds making dazzling patterns in the sky, and I was up there, surrounded by true natural beauty in all its wonder. In that moment it felt as if time had slowed down and it was all there just for me, so that I could bear witness to the glory of the natural world. I have felt moments like that before, and it's as if each time I encounter nature face-to-face, it adds a little bit more precious time to my stay on Earth.

I set my sights back toward Mother Earth's green pastures and angled the plane down.

But I couldn't see the runway.

How the hell was I supposed to land when I couldn't see the runway?

I could taste the adrenaline in my mouth. And yet, it didn't taste like *fear*. It still tasted like *thrill*. Like this was just another unexpected bump in my latest adventure. I was full of confidence.

But that runway . . . I couldn't judge the depth. I had to pull up.

"Bill, what are you doing? You were there!"

"I couldn't see it! I'm coming around again."

Around I went. Of course, since we were getting all this beautiful footage during golden hour, the sun was setting *fast.* I was running out of light.

I came in for a second shot at the landing. I still couldn't judge the runway. "Shit," I said, "I don't like this." Again, I pulled up and went for another go-around.

By now, it was close to dark. In all my training, I was yet to land a taildragger unassisted—and that was during the day. If I couldn't land the plane during the day, how the hell was I going to do it in the dark?

Again, the taste of adrenaline, urging me on. *I can do this,* I told myself. More than I *can,* I *have* to. The light was almost gone, and it wasn't like they could send someone up to take the controls and bring it in safely. This was my moment. *Let's go, Bill!*

I came in for my third attempt and somehow, I brought it in for a smooth landing. No ground loops, no rolls, no damage. I don't know how I did it, but I did. Mother Earth welcomed me back. I had lived another day, survived another adventure, and my heart was full like never before.

The third experience I remember so vividly

from *The American Sportsman* was one I look back on with memories not of touching the face of nature but of defiling nature.

I should preface this story by noting that it is confronting, upsetting, and sad. Frankly, it is the greatest regret of my life. I have survived many stunts and foolish impulses; I've laughed them off by saying I should have been killed but was lucky not to. In this story, if I had been killed, I dare say I would have deserved it.

This episode took place between the other two I mentioned, but I wanted to close with it because it serves as a reminder of one of the lowest moments of my life and, I hope, as admonition for others to avoid following in my footsteps and disrupting the beauty of the world.

While shooting a TV pilot called *Alexander the Great* (with Adam West, who would later become TV's *Batman*), I had learned how to fire a bow and arrow. Later, one of the episodes of *Star Trek* called for Captain Kirk to show his archery skills. I did additional training with some archers, who set up a target for us to practice on between scenes. I got quite good at it and later even competed at a Pro/Am tournament in Detroit. I didn't win any competitions, but I didn't embarrass myself either.

After *Star Trek* went off the air, *The American Sportsman* once again booked me for an episode. They knew of my interest in archery and wanted to take me hunting. Not only was I into archery but I was foolishly imbued with romantic notions of hunting. You could say I thought man's place within nature was to conquer it, not, as I now feel, to love it and bear witness to its beauty. When the producers asked if I'd like to hunt a Kodiak bear with nothing but a bow and arrow, I didn't think twice.

They took me to Anchorage, Alaska. As we arrived at the hunting camp, a stretcher was being taken out. On the stretcher was a dead hunter. He had been mauled to death by a bear. We were told that he had been in a hunting group that had gotten to within five hundred yards, at which distance they felt they could shoot the bear with a telescopic sight on a rifle. They were wrong. Not only did they miss in their first attempts, but the bear heard and saw them, and before they could get it, it was upon them and the man who pulled the trigger was dead. The others were lucky to escape with their lives.

I should have been terrified but I was emboldened. I scoffed at the idea of shooting a bear with a gun. How was that fair? If this is supposed to be a sport and you've got a high-powered sniper rifle, what chance does the bear have? For it to be a true battle, you would need to stalk your prey, get close enough to smell it (as it could surely smell you), and you'd have to use the same weapons our ancestors had when they hunted bears for food. You had to do it with a bow and arrow, not this uncivilized rifle.

How naive I was. Neither method is acceptable. Both are anathemas to nature. I should have known better.

At the time, I was fascinated by the bow and arrow. It was a perfect expression of how man could harness instruments from the wild and turn them into a force greater than himself. I had mostly used a longbow made from yew wood. Yew is ideal for building bows because of the combination of tensions from different parts of its trees. The exterior sapwood, found just below the bark, can stretch under tension, while the heartwood, from the center of the tree, holds very stable during compression, making it ideal for the belly of the bow.

There were at least two ways of shooting a bow that I knew of. You could have a sight—not unlike a gun sight—or you could do it free-form, which is what I opted for. (Again, these idiotic romantic notions of hunting were swimming in my head.) When you shoot free-form, you develop a feeling for where the arrow is going to go; it's a bit like golfing, in that regard: you visualize where the ball is going to go, and you hit it to send it along that trajectory. The great golfers can get the ball to follow the exact line they want and often land within just a few feet of the hole, or sometimes even in it.

The trajectory of an arrow fired from a bow is similar: you aim and fire it and it rises a few feet into the air, carried by the energy released by the pulling of the string. As it flies, the arrow meets air resistance and settles into an arc, where gravity eventually pulls it down. If you are close to your target, you have to allow for the arrow to rise when it is fired; if your target is farther away, you must account for the arc and gravity eventually pulling the arrow down. If you're shooting from more than forty or fifty yards, you're essentially aiming into the air and using your well-practiced skills to judge the angle and distance correctly so the arrow will land more or less where you're aiming.

Leaving aside the questions I didn't ask myself about whether it was right to hunt a beautiful, innocent creature, I was absorbed by the mechanics of the device. How these ancient archers could take a bent piece of wood, add string to it, and turn it into a projectile weapon that could kill from hundreds of yards away was a staggering feat in my mind. I had also been introduced to the recurve bow, which had originally been developed by the Mongols about 1,000 BCE and was making a modern comeback.

The modern recurve bow is more mechanical than a curved wooden longbow, but it is lighter, more agile, and more accurate. Today, it is the only bow used in Olympic archery. When you pull back the string and the arrow, you come to a rest and need to anchor the arrow; this is done usually by keeping the back of the arrow pressing up against your mouth and repeating the same movement each time you pull back so you can fire in a straight line and not send the arrow off in a haphazard motion.

You won't believe this but it's true: the hunting expert they paired me with was a fellow named Fred Bear. Fred Bear had been a pioneer in manufacturing bows and had become an avid hunter. He had arranged for three cameramen, a guide, and me to venture into the Kodiak Archipelago so we could hunt a Kodiak bear. We weren't allowed to locate the bear from the air, so we had to stalk it through the forbidding Alaskan wilderness. The area was very dense; great thickets of woods made it very difficult to spot any bears.

After ten arduous days, our guide spotted a bear in the distance. "He knows we're here," the guide told me ominously. "Just know, when he gets here, he's likely to stand up. He'll be nine or ten feet tall and will weigh fifteen hundred pounds, maybe more." Yikes.

"You'll have your arrow," he reminded me. Easy for him to say; he had a rifle!

Fifty yards ahead of us there was a gap in the thick copse of woods. In the other direction was a dry riverbed; behind us were more trees. The expectation was that the bear would slide out from underneath the woods and appear in the gap, then come toward us on all fours, assuming he hadn't spotted us. (If he'd spotted us, he would make a break for the open tundra to either get away or try to encircle us.) I had two arrows; one stuck in the ground, the other in my bow, ready to fire. Out of the corner of my eye, I caught sight of our guide with the rifle. *He was shaking.*

Suddenly, the bear made a move. He stood up in the distance—and he was every bit as tall and as terrifying as I'd been warned. But he didn't come toward us; he started running on all fours *around* the gap, heading for the woods behind us. He'd seen us! Our plan had gone completely out the window. The bear wasn't going to present himself to us (which even then would be a challenge, to say the least!); he was going to flank around us and pop up from behind! Acting on nothing but impulse and intuition, I fired an arrow at the bear while he was running. The arrow arced up, came down, and lodged itself in the bear's back.

To reiterate, this was one of the lowest chapters of my life, and I still hate myself for what I did that day.

The specific hunting arrows I was armed with were made of two razor blades, allowing them to cut into whatever they hit. What we knew but what the innocent bear couldn't possibly know was that the more he moved, the deeper into his body the blades would cut, until eventually they found an artery, and the poor thing bled to death—which can take hours.

The guide looked on in horror. "We've got a bad bear," he said in hushed tones. He was wounded and angry, and we were on foot in *his* woods. He had the advantage over us. "A wounded bear," the guide told me, "is the most dangerous animal of all."

We waited for what seemed like an eternity, too frightened to move, lest we give away our position. After a little longer, the guide ventured out slowly and deliberately into the woods and found the bear. It had died. It was a triumphant moment, captured on film and broadcast to millions. I got caught up in the moment. I even had his head and hide turned into a rug and had it in a country house I owned for twenty years. Over the years, the skin turned beige, and one of my dogs ate the bear's two-inch nails. I finally threw it out in disgust.

I wish I had taken a lesson from *Star Trek*'s "Prime Directive." As a concept of noninterference, it was both challenging and debatable. Should we avoid meddling, or should we consider intervening when doing so can avoid destruction? Some of the best *Star Trek* episodes involve breaking the Prime Directive, such as at the end of "Armageddon Game," in which Captain Kirk destroys the computer responsible for selecting people to be executed in a virtual war. Yet, ethically, who are we to say that our ideals are better than those we might seek to supplant? When it comes to animals in their natural state, however, I believe in the Prime Directive. I had no business being in that bear's habitat and taking its life.

To this day, I remain profoundly ashamed of what I did in the name of adventure. To go out into nature and see the splendor of creation in its natural habitat and *kill* it . . . I will carry that regret with me for the rest of my life. It is hard to believe, given what I'd like to think is my more sharpened consciousness today, that I would ever have found hunting for sport to be acceptable, let alone thrilling. The only excuse I can give myself is that it was the style at the time; after all, they gave out permits so you could hunt these creatures. We were perhaps less enlightened as a species but it's still a poor excuse. After all, something doesn't have to be illegal for you to know that it's wrong. Don't get me started on factory farming conditions, for example.

A friend told me of a trip he had taken to a nature preserve in Thailand in 1995. There was a group of monkeys swinging around an enclosure, but they were each chained from a collar. They could only swing about ten feet in any direction. He and the crowd thought nothing of it; when he thinks back on it today, it seems utterly barbaric to limit these creatures' movement like that. "How could we be okay with that?" he asked me. That is the same reaction I have to my time as a hunter, when I killed that beautiful Kodiak bear. How could I have been okay with that? What was I thinking? Where was my humanity?

In my attempt to broaden my understanding of the natural world, I am happy to report that I have since been near many more of this planet's heavenly creatures but only to admire them; never to hunt. And still I am gripped by a desire to put myself as close to adventure and danger as possible, just for a chance to glimpse more of the grandeur of life and nature on this blue marble.

On a trip not that long ago, I was in Africa with my family for a nature tour. One night, I was awakened by a strange sound. It was a crunching; no, not crunching, *munching*. *What on earth was that?* I sat up in bed and through the window, right outside, plain as day, was a huge elephant. We knew there were elephants in the area and had been warned to just give them their space. Doors in these sleeping huts were not locked because, for all their intelligence, elephants can't open doors. I was absolutely mesmerized by this beautiful creature as it *munched away on the thatched hut of our roof.* Yet, I didn't fear that it was going to eat its way into the hut. I don't know what came over me; I wanted to be closer.

Before I knew it, I found myself outside,

accompanied only by a small flashlight, wearing nothing but my underwear and a big boyish grin, watching this elephant, in awe of its size and grace. I later heard the story recounted by my daughter Melanie, who was awakened by what she thought were lightning flashes. She paused for the thunder but didn't hear anything; a few moments later, there were more flashes, yet still no thunder. *Do they have silent lightning storms in Botswana?* she thought. Melanie's husband, Joel, woke up next to her just as she twigged to what was going on.

"Is everything okay? Is something out there?" he asked groggily. "It's fine," Melanie replied, "it's just my dad." She couldn't see me, but after years of learned experience, she knew exactly what I was up to. Where nature called, I followed.

The elephant cantered away from our huts, and naturally, I gave chase. I followed this brilliant beast down toward a river, the water gleaming incandescently in the moonlight. The elephant wandered off into a clearing, but I was transfixed by a new sight: hippos. Hippos! They were sitting in the water, munching, looking around, just going about their business. I was transfixed. The size of those things!

Later that morning, back at camp, word had gotten around about my unscheduled, unsupervised expedition. In fact, one of the guides had radioed ahead to the next campsite to let his colleagues know, "We have a crazy man on the tour." When my family learned that a tourist had been killed by a lion on one of these tours a couple of years earlier, they were not happy with me.

At breakfast, one of the guides sat me down, like a parent disciplining a rambunctious child.

"Are you aware that hippos are the most dangerous mammals on the African continent?"

"I knew they were dangerous, yes."

"They are large and aggressive. They weigh six thousand pounds and they have very sharp teeth."

"I understand."

"I know you are the captain," he said, with only half a grin, "but we cannot continue the tour unless you follow the rules."

Chastened, but still giddy from my experience, I laughed it off and agreed to follow the rules.

Two days later, we were at another camp, eating lunch at a large communal dining table in a tent. Suddenly, another tourist raced in. "You've got to see this!" he implored to anyone silly enough to follow him, and then disappeared back out of the tent.

Having learned my lesson, I stayed in the tent. I never found out what he had seen that was so compelling.

Yeah right.

Quick as lightning (or a flashlight), I was out of there.

What I saw was at once dangerous and alluring. Right across a large lawn was a stunning, elegant lioness. She was seemingly heading back to her pride, which would have been some distance away. She moved so gracefully, safe in the knowledge that she had no predators around. I don't know if she saw us, but if she did, she certainly knew she had nothing to fear. On the other hand, she could easily have made her way across the lawn and killed me at a moment's notice. She didn't, or you wouldn't be reading this book, and somehow, as always, in that moment, I felt impervious to the idea of danger.

There is beauty to witness, and I wasn't going to miss a moment of it. Perhaps I was being reckless; I certainly don't recommend many of the things I have done. All I can tell you is to smell those roses, to look closer at every person and every object and every vista and scene and circumstance you encounter. There is beauty all around us; we just have to open our eyes and look for it.

— CHAPTER 8 —

YOUR PLACE IN THE UNIVERSE

I don't have a god. I don't believe there is a deity in the heavens with a unique, individual plan for everything on Earth below and the stars above. If you have those beliefs, that is your right and if it works for you, that's wonderful. While I am not religious, I consider myself *spiritual.* Spiritual is sometimes just another term for smoking pot but not going to church or synagogue. I believe in the universe. I believe that somehow, in ways we just haven't figured out yet, we are all connected. There are too many coincidences, too many similarities. We are made of star stuff. We are connected by the same bonds as every living thing in the cosmos. The absence of an answer for all of life's questions does not indicate that there is no answer; it just means we haven't found it yet.

I have been thinking a lot lately about my place in the universe. Was it happenstance? Is there some reason my life has taken the specific path it has?

I have three teenage granddaughters. Each

is unique. In their own ways, they are all in the process of trying to discover who they are and what they want to do. To me, that can seem like a blessing and a curse at the same time. At their ages, I was lucky in two significant ways. First, I *knew* what I wanted to be. From the time I first performed at six years old, I knew I never wanted to do anything else, and fortunately I had some natural abilities that I was able to hone. Second, and perhaps most crucial, I was given the freedom to be who and what I wanted to be.

This was not common at the time. In the post-war years, families like mine, descended from European émigrés and holding fast to their value systems, usually had preordained paths for their children to follow. Get a modicum of education so you can survive in the real world; follow your father into the family business; build a life and family of your own; pass your own version of that down to your offspring. Certainly, it was expected that I would follow my father into the suit-making business, but in a moment of cosmic fortune, I broke free of that path and my parents allowed me to do so.

In light of my desire to break away from the mold carved out by my parents, I was surprised that at one point, each of my daughters decided she might want to follow her father into the family business, which was now show business. My daughter Leslie never misses a chance to remind me of how quickly she was turned off to the profession. In the *Star Trek* season one episode "Miri," the *Enterprise* finds a planet that is seemingly a duplicate of Earth, but where the only inhabitants left are children who have survived a deadly plague. So, we needed a bunch of kids. Gene Roddenberry volunteered his two daughters, Darleen and Dawn; Grace Lee Whitney (who played Yeoman Janice Rand) and I also got in on the act with her son Scott and my daughters Leslie and Lisabeth. Director Vincent McEveety also brought in his nephew Steven.

Leonard Nimoy, perhaps wisely, decided to keep his own children out of the spotlight. Neither followed him into acting, but his son, Adam, has become an accomplished television and film director. His documentary *For the Love of Spock*, made about his father, is a beautiful and touching piece of cinema. Leonard's daughter, Julie, has also found a calling behind the camera. She and her husband, David Knight, recently produced and directed a powerful documentary about Leonard's battle with COPD.

I thought having two of my kids in *Star Trek* with me (Melanie was too young) would be fun, but for Leslie, it was the opposite. In order for her to be in the episode, Gloria and I had to pull her out of a day camp she was really enjoying. The episode called for the planet's inhabitants to appear as if they'd been eking out an existence by scrounging and foraging, so they had to be dirty. While there truly is no business like show business, it is not always the most glamorous of professions. Eight-year-old Leslie did not enjoy having dirt thrown on her before every take. "By the end of the fourth day," she recalls, "I just remember wanting to go home, to go back to camp. I was sobbing and *that's* when you brought me closer to the camera for my close-up!" She was not a happy camper that day.

Five-year-old Lisabeth (she's the one I pick up and hold late in the episode) wasn't bothered by the dirt, but she didn't appreciate the gag I played on her when I pretended to be dying of some disgusting disease and showed her my arm, which was made up to look like the plague had begun to eat away at my flesh. She cried at first, and then scolded me when I told her I was kidding around. Ah, the misguided things we do to try to make our children laugh.

My youngest daughter, Melanie, dabbled in acting herself but fell out of love with it; she wound up thriving in a career in clothing and fashion. Somehow, the garment district genes of both her mother and her father came full circle in her chosen vocation. The synchronicity of it all is beautiful to behold.

We filmed the "Miri" episode at Desilu Culver Studios in Culver City, making use of the incredible RKO Forty Acres backlot (a.k.a. the Back Forty). The Back Forty is sadly no more, as real estate in that area of Los Angeles became too expensive to maintain such a large backlot; it was turned into an office park in the 1970s. In 1966, though, the television business was booming and made use of all manner of backlot sets. *Star Trek* filmed on the Back Forty many times, including for the original pilot, "The Cage," and famous scenes from "The City on the Edge of Forever," "Errand of Mercy," and others. "Miri" was shot on the same set used for Mayberry on *The Andy Griffith Show*, which was just a couple of pretend blocks away from the full-scale exterior sets used in *The King of Kings*; *King Kong*; *The Garden of Allah*; *Tarzan*; and later *Gomer Pyle, U.S.M.C.* and *Hogan's Heroes*.

It may not have been a tremendous experience for Leslie and Lisabeth, but I was so excited to be able to bring them into my make-believe world, however briefly. Parents don't always get to enjoy that kind of experience, and while I am mostly relieved none of them left themselves at the mercy of the entertainment industry, we are all richer for the experience.

What strikes me as I look back on my own time as a teenager who decided to follow a different path from the rest of his family and go into the arts is that it wasn't all that dramatic (pun intended). Once I knew I enjoyed performing,

I didn't struggle with the idea that I wouldn't be able to do it. It sounds strange, given my upbringing and my father's expectation of my following in his footsteps, but I did not lie awake at night worried about my choices or defying my parents. I did not struggle with the cosmic questions of who I was and what I wanted to do. I was constantly involved in amateur theatricals, whether through school or community theater. It pleased my mother because she loved to see me perform; my father must have known something was brewing because he always approached these plays with a degree of caution. Yet for me, it never felt like a burning desire; it just felt like this is what I was doing and would continue to do; no ifs, ands, or buts.

Sure enough, in my later adolescent years, as I approached the end of high school, I walked into my parents' bedroom one night and said, simply, "I'd like to try to be an actor." My father was more astonished than upset or wrathful. He alerted me to the challenging circumstances I was facing: I was lower-middle class, an economic reality that did not allow me to become an actor. To be an actor, you must either be rich enough that you can do whatever you want, or so poor that it doesn't matter, because your only other option is collecting tin cans to survive, so you may as well try to be an actor.

I had a place in a lower-middle-class structure.

I wasn't supposed to stray outside of that; I was supposed to complete my studies and put my shoulder to the wheel to help my family. It was a very traditional path. As a dutiful member of the family, you were supposed to support its stability and structure. My father was not overwhelmingly successful, but he made a good enough living to provide for us and help the rest of his family with whatever was left over.

On Sundays, my father would take me to one or more of his siblings' homes in Montreal. We would sit around for a couple of hours; they'd eat bagels and cream cheese (lox if there was enough money that week) and maybe a cup of milk, and talk about who was doing what to whom and how they all felt about it. As a kid in the 1930s, you didn't have an iPhone; you didn't have anything. You just sat there. Where your parents went, you went, and you were bored out of your mind. Jerry Seinfeld captured this idea perfectly in one of his stand-up routines: "When you're five and you get bored, you cannot support your body weight. . . . Adulthood is the ability to be totally bored and remain standing."

My father may not have loved it, but even he knew that there was no denying me at least the attempt to become an actor. I'm sure he expected that I'd give it a couple of years, feel that I'd been heard, fail, and then join him in the garment business. Being an actor was a high-risk proposition. It always has been, and nothing in that regard has ever really changed.

In looking back, what I find interesting—and I don't mean to be immodest; I was far from the only one in this boat—is that I found a way to succeed despite the challenges of life that can otherwise prevent some people from following their chosen calling. Many people today put off starting a family until well into their thirties; it gives them time to try out several careers and really "give it a shot" until they either succeed enough to support starting a family or pick up a new vocation that gives them the necessary stability to do so. I didn't have that luxury, but I was also never cognizant of it being an option.

In some ways, I think the combination of an actor's discipline and simply not knowing any better played a profound part in allowing me to forge a career while also raising children. It is easy (or easier, perhaps) to have a family when you have a solid career base beneath you. I never had that, and oddly, it simply did not occur to me that I could fail. Any obstacle or unexpected event in front of me was just part of life. In the case of having a family, it was a profoundly beautiful part of life. It just had to be nurtured and loved and supported financially.

Money was always tight for me and yet before I knew it, in my early twenties, I was married. Shortly thereafter, there was a baby, and then two, and then three. I don't remember Gloria and me ever planning to start or expand our family. We didn't look at the calendar or the budget and say, "Okay, we can have one kid now, then another in two years, and then we'll see if we want a third after that." Instead, one day, she told me, "I'm pregnant."

Gloria and I were married in 1956; the kids came along in 1958 (Leslie), 1961 (Lisabeth), and 1964 (Melanie). In February 1969, despite a valiant effort from Bjo and John Trimble (who had been successful in their push to get the show a third season a year earlier) and their gallant letter-writing campaigners, *Star Trek* was canceled. The following month, Gloria and I got divorced.

I moved out of our home in Beverly Hills and rented what I will describe charitably as a two-bedroom *house* in Studio City, so the girls could stay with me when it was my turn to look after them. I was responsible for supporting them, but now had to pay for two homes and had just lost my job. *Star Trek* hadn't paid overwhelmingly well, and there were no residuals back then, so I needed to move quickly to find a new source of income.

I was able to take a role on the summer stock circuit on the East Coast. As I wasn't going to be paid until after the first batch of performances, and with every spare penny going to take care of

Gloria and the kids, I didn't have enough money to fly (which was considerably more expensive in those days), so I resolved to drive coast to coast. I bought a very old pickup truck, installed a camper pod on top, and took off across the country, my Doberman, Morgan, my only companion.

I did thirteen weeks of summer stock and was relieved to be able to go home and see my daughters. The last performance was on a Saturday night, and on Sunday morning I was on the road, desperate to make it home to spend time with my girls during the upcoming Jewish holiday of Yom Kippur. Early in the trip, I stopped at a pay phone to check in with my agent. I was hoping he had work for me; he didn't, but he had *something*.

"Rose Kennedy wants to invite you to a party at the Kennedy Compound." Wow, a party at the Kennedy Compound. There wasn't a job, but those parties were legendary; attending would be a special experience. Unfortunately, the party was later that week, and there was no way I was going to delay my return. I hadn't seen my kids in three months.

On the second day of my return trip, I checked in with my agent again. "Rose Kennedy really wants you to attend this party. She loved *Star Trek*."

"No, no, I can't. I've got to get home to my kids."

"They'll send an airplane for you!"

"Please tell Mrs. Kennedy I am thankful, but I just cannot make it."

I was just so desperate to get home. Only later did I realize that if I'd been thinking more clearly, I could have had them send a plane to pick me and Morgan up on the road (we were in Albuquerque by this point), dropped by LA to pick up my kids, and brought them all to Massachusetts for the party. But I was too blinded by emotion and fatigue. I could not see past my immediate need to support my family and stave off poverty and starvation.

Through all of that, it had never occurred to me not to be an actor, which in hindsight is somewhat absurd, given the abject financial circumstances in which I had found myself on numerous occasions. I always managed to pay the rent, even though I was not always working and had occasionally come to the point of starvation between jobs. In hindsight, there is a certain one-dimensional quality to how I got through those difficult years without any hint of self-examination, of wondering if this was how my life was supposed to turn out.

I am reminded of Bertolt Brecht's *The Caucasian Chalk Circle*, in which Grusha finds the governor's son, Michael, abandoned. She does not process the enormously complicated emotions that would go into adopting a child; she merely reasons, "Since no one else will take you, son, I must take you." Grusha then takes on the responsibility of raising this child she has found. My life was similar in an unexamined sort of way. When there was rent to be paid, I found a way to pay it; when there were mouths to be fed, I found a way to feed them.

In the 1970s, one of the ways I did this was to make appearances on game shows. It was a good gig, and I had a lot of fun, frequently playing the fool on national television, all the while knowing that doing so was providing for my precious family.

Perhaps the greatest times I had were in my many appearances on the *Pyramid* game show with Dick Clark and later Bill Cullen, both terrific guys. I had a look at some of the old clips and could not help but laugh my ass off.

The show was filmed on Saturdays in New York. I was living in LA, so I would take the red-eye on Friday night, arrive Saturday morning, and take a taxi to the studio. I'd land around nine or ten in the morning, and then we'd do five shows in one day. It was a very taxing experience, not to mention how I had to run up three or four flights of stairs to my dressing room to change clothes, then back down to shoot the next episode. (We couldn't wear the same clothes, since the episodes had to appear as if they'd been taped on different days.) So, when you find these clips on YouTube (and they're available—that's where I found them!), keep in mind the jetlag and scheduling mania that were ever-present in my appearances on this game show.

First clip: me dancing on *The $25,000 Pyramid*. The contestant opposite me was fantastic. Admittedly, I wasn't great with my dancing styles, but boy, she picked up on them so fast. I started in the first few seconds by trying to describe the dances, but soon I was up out of my chair and moving my body and feet as fast as I could to convey them: waltz, Charleston, polka, belly dancing, ballet, square dancing . . . We ran out of time on the minuet, and truthfully, even with another ten seconds, that one might have stumped us, but hey, six answers in thirty seconds was pretty impressive on that show.

Second clip: me being ridiculous on *The $10,000 Pyramid*. For a gag, the producers told me to be both host *and* contestant. With energy and madness flowing through me, I flung myself between the two chairs. The funniest thing was that as I went back and forth, I had access to the answers, because they were on the host's screen, and yet I was trying so hard to avoid looking at them; I wanted to try to answer the clues myself. But I couldn't. I was just too manic. I almost broke the set from bouncing up and down between the chairs. Then even when I looked at the answers, my mind was racing so fast that I couldn't get the words out of my mouth.

Final clip: me losing my mind on *The $20,000 Pyramid*. You can find this one under the apt title "William Shatner blows $20K for a contestant." The one major rule on *The $20,000 Pyramid* was that you couldn't use any of the words in the prompt; rather, you had to use other words in your clues to get your partner to guess the prompt. In my case, the prompt was THINGS THAT ARE BLESSED. So, what do I blurt out? "The blessed—" Bang, I just cost someone a shot at $20,000!

In his incredible 2021 memoir, *All About Me!*, Mel Brooks tells a terrific story about making *Blazing Saddles*. When trying to decide if he was really going to go through with some of the more extreme parts of the film (punching a horse; a bunch of bean- and coffee-fed cowboys farting their butts off around a campfire), Mel asked John Calley, then head of production at Warner Bros., for advice. Calley told Mel, "If you're going to go up to the bell, ring it." Great advice.

Having accidentally found myself at the proverbial bell by screwing up the clue for the contestant, logically, there was only one appropriate response here: with adrenaline, sleep deprivation, and humiliation coursing through my veins, I lost my damn mind, and I rang that bell. I pounded on the winner's circle barrier, then I threw my chair out of the circle! Dick Clark had to go retrieve it for me. If you're going to lose your mind on national television, you shouldn't half-ass it. Ring the bell.

To this day, I continue to love working, and I often jump at opportunities to keep flexing my creative muscles in different areas, including commercials and other promotions. If you were watching TV anywhere during Medicare open enrollment, you may have seen me in an ad for the Medicare Coverage Helpline, which provides information about supplemental Medicare Advantage Plans and connects you to providers, should you wish to purchase a plan. When I was asked to do the commercial, I looked into the program and felt satisfied that it could be helpful for some folks and save them some money. What embarrassed me a little is that there are just so many of those commercials. There's me; there's Jimmie Walker; Joe Namath seemed to do a hundred of them. It was as if they'd scrolled down the Screen Actors Guild roster and threw darts at a bunch of names.

Every so often a commercial comes along, and as an actor you must decide if it's innocuous enough that it doesn't do any harm to those watching it or to your reputation. I fully admit, it's a fine line sometimes. I've done commercials for sleep apnea gear (which I've used), law firms that have helped the little guy against big companies, and, of course, I was the Priceline Negotiator.

Film stars used to do commercials in other countries for big buckets of money because they knew they'd never be seen in America, but now, with the internet and social media, information moves at an incredible speed. No one is safe, and you have to determine if it's worth it. (As an aside, Harvey Keitel reprised his Winston Wolf role from *Pulp Fiction* for a series of British insurance commercials, and they're fantastic! Everyone should see them.)

(As another aside, everyone should *also* see the outtakes of Orson Welles doing a commercial for Paul Masson champagne: he was completely drunk and the footage was utterly unusable. As always, consult YouTube.)

Many years ago, I was invited to the house of actor Edward G. Robinson for a dinner party. His house felt like a replica of the Guggenheim Museum: he had one of the greatest private collections of French impressionist paintings in the world, including works by Paul Cézanne, Henri de Toulouse-Lautrec, and Vincent van Gogh. Later in the evening, the two of us were having a drink and I asked him about those famous Maxwell House Coffee commercials he had done. "Ed," I said, "you're such a versatile actor. You speak seven languages. You're one of the talents of your generation. Why are you doing coffee commercials?"

Without a word, he merely gestured to the gorgeous works of art that adorned the walls of his Beverly Hills mansion.

So, when you see my face pop up on an obscure commercial, have a think about whether a Medicare Advantage Plan might work for you, and remember the great wisdom of Edward G. Robinson.

It is a point of pride to me that I have never missed work; I have never not appeared for a performance. My discipline as an actor came from an adage from back in my radio days, which is that if you're not five minutes early, you're late. Was that discipline, combined with my inability to see any other path for myself, a measure of knowing my place in the universe and the universe providing that path? I truly cannot say this with any certainty, although I have remarked on numerous occasions that I feel the universe is looking out for me.

We can call it luck or chance or fate, but sometimes lightning really does strike. The mere fact that we know Einstein's theories or Mozart's compositions is proof that cream does rise to the top. In my own profession, I always looked up to Sir Laurence Olivier and Marlon Brando. Brando was the epitome of Method acting, relatively new at the time, which is centered around calling on painful memories and life experiences to emote in a devastatingly real fashion. He strove for absolute reality in his performances, and from something deep inside him, perhaps psychological trauma, he was uniquely imbued to deliver that reality. That was his purpose. There is something so human about that. The fortune that his gift brought him surely helped, but we're talking about a guy who used his Oscar as a doorstop, so acclaim did not appear to be his motivating factor. This was who he was; he had a skill and was able to show it off and perfect it. In fact, in Brando's later life, he had mastered it so completely that he grew tired of the profession and supposedly considered it "child's play."

Olivier, on the other hand, was a technically trained actor. Legend has it that while on the set of *Marathon Man*, Dustin Hoffman described a scene he had performed in which his character had stayed up for three days and nights. When asked by Olivier how he had prepared for the scene, Hoffman replied, "I stayed up for three days and nights." Olivier is reported to have retorted, "My boy, why don't you just try acting?"

Olivier loved every aspect of his craft; he especially enjoyed makeup. It was apparently said that "When Sir Larry comes onstage, he is preceded by a nose," or words to that effect. Olivier came from the opposite end of the acting spectrum as Brando. With Brando, emotion—primal emotion—was everything; for Olivier, the truth was in the craft itself.

In my earlier days as an actor, I was privileged to see Olivier onstage. I don't remember the name of the play, but he portrayed a down-on-his-luck character with a menial job. There was one moment—blink and you'd miss it—in which he looked at his watch. I remember sitting in the audience, thinking, *Why is he looking at his watch? Is he bored? Is he waiting for intermission, for a bathroom break?* And then it occurred to me: he was showing the audience his cheap watch. It was the smallest of details, almost impossible to see unless you were in the first few rows, but it was a critical part of his character, and Olivier had thought of every facet and had found a way to communicate each of them to the audience. I was astonished, and it renewed my resolve to work even harder at my craft.

All actors have "gone dry" at one time or another, meaning they forget their lines onstage. It happened to me during a performance; I walked into the wings and asked the stage manager for the line, got it, then walked back out and performed it. I later asked a friend in the audience if he'd seen me leave the stage; it had happened so casually that he didn't remember it! One night, Olivier went dry and didn't return to the stage for five years. He was so frightened of it happening again. I found that upsetting but also comforting because it showed Olivier's humanity. Brando's came out in all manner of ways—in performances and then later in somewhat bizarre interviews and appearances; Olivier's came out in his fears. He was as fragile as the rest of us. To me, it served as a reminder to just "go for it," because even the best can lose themselves at times.

I never met either Brando or Olivier, although I can see Brando's old house from mine, and Olivier and I had many mutual friends because of his work in the Canadian theater. He and Christopher Plummer had been acquainted. While Brando and Olivier were my idols and indirect influences on my career, I can say with fond recall that Chris Plummer was instrumental in my early leaps. He was a couple of years older than me and a fellow Canadian; we had met in the Montreal theater circuit. Chris was playing the leads and I was playing supporting characters and often understudying him. He was a tremendously talented person across many disciplines. He could play piano; he could sing; he was an avid tennis player (and I envied how good he looked in his tennis togs!). He had an unerring ability to modulate his voice to produce a completely different timbre and tone, depending on the part.

I understudied Chris a lot at the Stratford Shakespeare Festival in Ontario. One night, he got sick before a performance of *Henry V*, and I had to go on for him, mostly unrehearsed. I managed to get through the show, and it helped my career immensely to have filled his shoes.

From there, I started to get bigger roles and had more of a presence in the touring companies. Many years later, I had the pleasure of working with Chris mano a mano in *Star Trek VI: The Undiscovered Country*. He had the delicious role of Klingon General Chang, and I loved every second of our work together. He was a true artist and gentleman. I miss him.

There may have been other Oliviers and Brandos waiting in the wings who had the talent but not the right timing. We may never know. In 2019, Danny Boyle directed a film called *Yesterday*, in which a young musician wakes up one day to find he is the only person who knows any of the Beatles' songs; it is as if they have just been erased from existence and he alone can recall them. He takes to writing and recording as many of them as he can remember, and soon becomes celebrated as the greatest individual songwriter of all time. It is a lovely film, and perhaps worth the price of admission alone for a beautiful scene with a certain Beatle who, in this timeline, never became famous. (That's all I'll say.) However, the original screenplay had a very different story and message behind it.

In the original draft of what was then called *Cover Version*, written by Jack Barth, the lead character (also Jack), who wakes up as the only person to remember the Beatles' songs, does not meet with success. He may have the songs, but he is in the wrong place at the wrong time. The screenplay's thesis was that it takes more than just talent; it takes a confluence of events all colliding at the same time to rise to the top. It wouldn't have made for as charming a film, so I can understand why Richard Curtis rewrote it the way he did, but for me, it is a more interesting examination of the path each of us might find for ourselves.

I think of the choices my grandkids have. They have the world at their feet. Nothing is impossible. There are no prearranged lives for them to live. Yet all this opportunity can cause consternation. When you have so many options, how do you pick the one or ones that are right for you? How do you know your place in the universe?

I have been blessed with five grandchildren: two boys and three girls. The boys are older and married, and one has a child of his own. I have watched them grow from mischievous young boys to curious adolescents to two of the finest human beings I know. They are successful at their jobs and have married two wonderful women. They are fulfilled and happy in their lives, and I am deliriously happy for them that they have found their places and are positively thriving.

My granddaughters are in the process of discovering how they fit into this world. One of them is a natural athlete. It is in her bones. Her hand-eye coordination is first-rate, and so at a young age, she gravitated to tennis. Young children are often able to try several different activities, and her parents had encouraged her interest in this sport. As it happens, she was gifted with a tennis racket and has since become something of a prodigy. She has competed in various tournaments, a number of which she has won, and could very well move up the rankings on the professional circuit one day.

But she is torn. She has devoted perhaps half her life so far to perfecting her game and her abilities, but she is keenly aware of what she has lost in that trade-off. She has missed out on parties and social events with her friends, and knows all too well that she may be missing out on elements of her adolescence that she simply cannot get back. I do not envy her this struggle but I admire her cognition: she is truly aware of this semi-existential crisis she is facing and continues to weigh up the pros and cons daily, trying to determine where her head and her heart might take her, or where she might want to take them. Without tennis, she is already an exceptional human being. Her brain will carry her; her savvy will carry her; her looks will even carry her, should she want to use them as part of a career. She may yet go on with her tennis or use it as a springboard to academia by means of a sports scholarship. But she struggles with the freedom of having choices.

Another of my grandchildren is also figuring out her path. She is gifted intellectually and knows that she wants to put her brain to some sort of scholarly pursuit. Right now, her mind is set on medical research. Even if she doesn't know where exactly her pursuits will lead, her innate desire for knowledge will give her a profession. There is perhaps a degree of comfort in that for her.

My eldest granddaughter is in the process of figuring out where the next chapter of her life might take her. Hers is a multifaceted and multi-talented personality. She has too many choices, and that can be daunting. As of this writing, she is in an undergraduate university in the South and has not enjoyed her time there. She has been accepted to a top university and must decide if she wants to travel there to continue her studies. If she chooses that path, will she find what she is looking for? I simply don't know. I am comforted by knowing that even though she is at times stifled by having so many options, she *has* those options in front of her.

I consider myself lucky that I knew what I wanted to be and was not gripped by any ambivalence, but it's easier to consider yourself lucky when you've been successful. I can see, however, that knowing so completely what you want could turn into a source of confusion and angst. Consider the plight of someone who believes they have been born with a purpose. A musician who is naturally gifted, for example, and who by exercising those gifts has all the potential in the world. Life intervenes—a breadwinning family member dies and suddenly, this person cannot be a musician. The dream is taken away from them; they must take on a different vocation, *any vocation,* really, to allow life to continue. That is not to say that you cannot pivot and still find happiness, but you would be entitled to feel that life had dealt you a rough hand.

Likewise, for those who have a burning desire to take a certain path, there are sacrifices, as my tennis-prodigy granddaughter has discovered. You may find yourself separated from many aspects of the culture around you because of your dedication to your one true goal. Even if you succeed, you may have left something behind along the way. Consider the opposite outcome, too: someone who toils night and day to achieve their long-held dreams, only to come up short. What do you do then? If you have no other skills, where do you go next? These are unenviable positions, and yet for many, they are the byproducts of a changing economic system that, between the ubiquitousness of technology, the rise of automation, the gig economy, and lower social mobility, gives newer generations more theoretical choices but fewer vocational certainties.

In some ways, I was relieved when my three daughters had lost interest in acting, but you could say I had a "scare" that there might be a hint of the acting bug in the next generation. A few years ago, I went to one of my granddaughters' high school theatrical productions, in which she had a sizable role. From the moment she hit the stage, the audience was captivated. I glanced in her father's direction and we shared a look as if to say, "Oh shit, she's so good. She might actually want to do this for a living!" She had the spark, the X factor, the talent. Fortunately, she, too, fell out of love with acting. I consider that a good thing, given everything I know about the industry.

My parents' generation, and to a lesser degree my own, raised their children to do what they did; later, with more wealth and stability, that seemed to change. Many children born in the seventies and eighties were more likely to be told, "Do whatever you want," and sometimes, *"Don't* do what I did." "Don't be a doctor—everyone is always calling you for free advice and you're dealing with blood and mess every day, and no one appreciates you." "Don't be a lawyer; there are too many lawyers."

Many children are told to "do what you love, be who you want to be," which to me is cliché, and yet there is truth to it. I guess I am somewhat hypocritical because I was relieved my children didn't become actors, while at the same time, I cannot imagine the trauma of going through life hating what you do.

I knew a person with a regular, workaday profession. She was so excited that she was going to be able to retire in a few years. I was perplexed. "What is so great about retirement?"

"Well," she told me, "when I'm retired, I'll finally be able to do what I really want to do." Hearing that made me so sad. She had worked for four decades, and was paid well, but each night she came home with the thought that she hated her job, looking forward to that distant day when she would finally have enough financial security to leave her disdained career in the dust. I know people need to work, but my goodness, my wish for you is that you at least don't have to do something you actively detest. I don't know what might have happened to me if I did something I hated for nine hours a day, then lathered, rinsed, and repeated the next day for decades on end. I know, however, that I would rather have sacrificed almost everything and toiled doing something I loved than lived securely in a life without contentment and fulfillment.

I was in New York City some years ago, having dinner at a steakhouse. I had seen a homeless fellow on the corner as I went to the restaurant and had decided to get some food to give him on my way back to my hotel. I ordered an additional piece of steak and had it wrapped in foil. I returned to the corner and approached the man.

"I was at the steakhouse up the street and had them cook up an extra piece for you," I said with a smile as I offered the food to him.

He looked at me with a hint of hesitation for a moment, then replied, "Is it rare or well-done?"

In some ways, I think that man was more certain of himself than anyone I have ever met. I admired his certitude. (Thankfully, the steak was medium, and he was content with the compromise.)

In the *Star Trek* episode "Balance of Terror," Dr. McCoy makes an impassioned plea to Captain Kirk: "In this galaxy, there's a mathematical probability of three million Earth-type planets. And in all the universe, three *million million* galaxies like this. And in all of that, and perhaps more, only one of each of us." That singular quality of each life is what I thought of when I met this homeless man, and I truly admire him. I'm not saying he was where he wanted to be, but he knew who he was. Whatever pitfalls and missteps he may have taken to lead him to this station in life, he had not lost that spark that made him the only version of himself in the universe.

In that vein, in late 2021, I visited Ticonderoga in upstate New York for a wonderful convention they call "Trekonderoga." At this convention, I held a "Chautauqua," which is sort of an educational exchange in which scholars or other speakers meet with a group of folks and discuss issues in any number of formats. I met with thirty or forty people from various backgrounds, each as interesting as the last.

At one point, I found myself speaking to the most fascinating individual I have ever met. His name is Mareach Angok, though he goes by the anglicized "Moe" for short. Moe had grown up in civil war–era South Sudan. He explained that as a child, he'd looked exactly like the kids we would see in foreign aid commercials, barely clothed, out under a blistering sun, malnourished, often engaged in physical labor meant for people twice his age and three times as strong.

With the fighting threatening their lives every day, Moe had set out with his mother, his sister, and a group of villagers for a perilous trek on foot from South Sudan to Ethiopia. They crossed treacherous rivers, slept in hideous conditions, and braved the harsh East African landscape over a period of months to finally make it to safety. They did all this barefoot, often having to pry thorns out of their aching feet with a knife. After they'd spent several years in Ethiopia, the war had moved closer to their new location, and they were forced to grab whatever possessions they could, including a herd of goats that Moe was responsible for, and make the arduous journey *back* to South Sudan.

After enduring countless horrors, Moe and another of his sisters were fortunate enough to make it into a refugee program run by Catholic Charities in conjunction with United States Citizenship and Immigration Services and were relocated to Rochester, Minnesota. Sitting in a basic apartment he shared with several others, Moe would watch American television—starting with *Sesame Street* and *The Price Is Right*, which in his native Dinka was "*amaar èe moñy deet-tè*," translating roughly into "The Old Man's Meeting."

Moe taught himself English by watching Big Bird, Bob Barker, and his new favorite program, *Star Trek*. Moe's love of the show spurred a fascination with engineering. He seized every opportunity he had to educate himself, attending school and spending most of his free time at the library, reading every book he could get his hands on. Today, Moe is Blue Origin's Senior Systems Design Integrator. Is that not the absolute epitome of human potential being realized?

I was so fascinated by Moe's incredible journey that I invited him to be a guest on my web talk show, *I Don't Understand*. The episode is only twenty-something minutes long, and they had to cut so much out because he and I spoke for almost an hour. I have encouraged Moe to write a memoir of his remarkable journey from rags to rocket ships, and I hope one day soon you'll be able to read all about his life. He is a true example of someone who had to fight every moment of his life and overcome incalculable odds to not only succeed but to thrive. Stories like Moe's give me hope for humanity when it can seem hard to come by.

Your place in the universe is whatever you make of it. I don't know how I got here, and I don't have any specific advice that could allow you to replicate my journey. All I can tell you is that I truly believe there is an entanglement at work in the universe, that we are all connected. Each time you open yourself up to that possibility, there's a little bit more on offer, a little bit more to explore. There is synchronicity in our universe; we may not be able to understand it, but opening our minds to this synchronicity allows us to better explore the greatest frontier of all: our shared connection to each other.

— CHAPTER 9 —

WHEN I'M GONE

I live in the San Fernando Valley. Often I find myself caught up, drinking in all the exquisite nature. Wide-eyed, I look out over the valley, mountains over here, clouds in the sky over there. Sometimes, just sometimes (this *is* LA, after all) there will be some rain, and the ground will take on a soft dampness. Intellectually, I understand it's just weather. But you know what? It's *not* just weather. It's beauty. It's the miracle of tectonic plates, of original volcanic material that hardened millennia ago, like the sugar on top of a crème brûlée. Then it shook, even just a little, and slipped. And it became a mountain. And from the peaks of the mountain, we got the slopes of the valley. From my house, I can see the majesty. The incredible engine of life, the story of Earth, the mystery of how it all happened. I will miss that beautiful simplicity. I will miss it all.

Because I'm going to die.

There is no getting around it; it is a fact. One day, hopefully not too soon, I will slip across that ever-so-narrow gap between life and death, and I will cease to be. I am terrified of it. I am scared to death . . . of death. I don't have the certitude of knowing what comes next. I would like to, but I expect to just *stop*. That will be the story of me. At my age, it is something I think about regularly.

I am blessed to know that some people will miss me when I am gone, but more and more, I think about what *I* will miss. I love life, every precious moment of it. I will miss it. I will miss the sun in the sky; I will miss voraciously tearing through the pages of a new book; I will even miss the hideous Los Angeles traffic, because it is part of the miracle of this ineffable world of ours. (It's not a great part, but it's all part of a rich tapestry, isn't it?)

I will miss my family. Their warmth, their laughter, the fullness of the bonds we have created and fostered over decades of trials, tribulations, triumphs, tragedies, and everything in between. I will miss what is yet to come. My granddaughter in Rome, for example. A few years ago, she was a frustrated teenage girl; she'd be at home, stewing in her room over the latest injustice to befall her, and the unfair nature of life that only adolescents can feel (to the exclusion of all others); and now she is a young woman, a beautiful orb of light, exploring the world, seeing all that it has to offer, and positively thriving. On one of our video calls, she began with "Hi, Papa! I want to go to Costa Rica!" There was a thirst in her voice. She couldn't wait another second to get out those words, to express the wonder she yearned to imbibe. What fascinations will she find at her next destination? What will become of her? What wonderful or tragic circumstances will she encounter in each chapter of her own life?

We can delve into the past and try to catch every detail and discovery of the present. We can read the news; we can study books. We can learn about the latest technology, dive into past eras, examine historical figures and events that have taken place on this young planet of ours. But we can only guess at what comes next. We can only imagine. Through my work, I have lived in the imaginations of some of the greatest writers of our time. I have glimpsed a possible future they have foretold. But I do not know what will become of my grandchildren or my great-grandchildren.

I will miss my darling Elizabeth; I will miss my dear and wonderful assistant and friend, Kathleen. I already miss things I did in my youth that I can no longer do. I can no longer ski and can only look back and hope I didn't miss an opportunity in my days on the slopes, playing in the snow, feeling the cold air in my lungs, and looking out over the vistas from high atop the mountains, formed perfectly by time and the miracle engine of the world, which will continue long after each of us leaves.

Just as I no longer ski, I am aware that there will come a day when I will no longer be able to ride a horse. On that day, I will lose a part of myself. During the writing of this book, I became aware of how much closer I am to that regretful day. My legs are weaker, and my breath is shorter, and as a result, one day when I was practicing with a horse, I fell off. It was as if it happened in slow motion. I have fallen off horses before. I've had horses fall on me! But this was different. I wondered if this was it. Was this my last ride?

I remember it so vividly and kept experiencing it so clearly, over and over again. The horse stumbled. I lurched forward. She must have thought I was going to stop, so she stopped. I was carried over her front and she jumped away; I saw her hooves go right by my face. And then, boom. I landed on the point of my shoulder. I cracked a couple of bones, and for a short while, I was in a sling. But my riding days were not done. I worked every day on my recovery and before too long, I was back in the saddle. Because I can't *not* do it.

If I'm aware that it's my final day when it inevitably comes, I will be filled with sadness and questions. Did I spend enough time with my family? With my friends? With my beloved horses, with my precious dogs? The saving grace of these thoughts is that when they do come into my head on any normal day, I take action. I go back to my horses. I play with my dogs. I tell my wife and my family and my friends that I love them. I offer a compliment to someone and see their face light up. I will miss all of that.

What will come next? Will I have a final revelation as I take my last breath? Will I see the answers to all my questions?

I am asked often about what I hope my "legacy" will be. I'm not sure I know what that means. Lin-Manuel Miranda, in his remarkable opus *Hamilton*, writes (and sings) as the titular character, "What is a legacy? It's planting seeds in a garden you never get to see." The musical asks the question, "When you're gone, who remembers your name? Who keeps your flame? Who tells your story?" I think the idea of a legacy is ephemeral. For most folks, it might be good for about three days. Maybe my grandchildren will be sad for a while: "Oh, Grandpa's gone." But then their lives will take over. "Let's go to the movies." "I have to write this paper." "I have to send a text to this handsome Italian boy . . ."

I don't think there is anything permanent about most legacies. Stories pass from memory. Statues are torn down. Buildings are renamed. Perhaps the real legacy is the continuation of the bonds you have spent a lifetime building. The passing on of your genes through your family. I don't have any male children, but the female genetic part of me is still going, which I find comforting and gratifying.

I have achieved some fame in my life (and some notoriety), and it is not so much that I desire to maintain this level of fame when I am gone (after all, I won't know any better), but I am aware that people have looked to me with questions. For many of them, for my family, those questions will exist after I no longer do, so how can I continue to answer them? I don't claim to have any wisdom, but if someone wants to know an answer to a question and I'm not around for them to ask, I have written many books and have tried to leave behind my thoughts and feelings across a lifetime of adventures. Is it enough?

Technology, that most double-edged of swords, may play a part in defining some of our legacies, what others can take from us after we have departed. Leonard Nimoy was able to reach the whole world with his last thoughts, thanks to Twitter. A few days before he died, he had summed up his feelings on life in an elegiac, most beautiful way through a tweet, sent out into the world: "A life is like a garden. Perfect moments can be had, but not preserved, except in memory. LLAP." (Live Long and Prosper.)

I thought a lot about legacy when Leonard died. He left us on a Friday. We had been kindred spirits when we'd met all those years ago. Two young Jewish boys—one from Montreal, one from Boston—trying to make our way in life and in art, standing at the helm of this strange science-fiction series that would come to define our lives.

As I circled the room at the charity event I was hosting in Florida (at the same time that his memorial service was taking place in Los Angeles), I found myself getting into deep conversations about the legacy of this great man, Leonard Nimoy. What would he be known for? "Well, he was Mr. Spock," people would tell me. Yes, he was, but he was so much more. He contributed to charity. He was there for his friends. He performed good deeds. Perhaps those are the best moments that can define someone's legacy, even if most will never know what they were. Good deeds. Helping someone cross the street. Being there for a friend, or a stranger. These deeds can reverberate. Maybe that person crossing the street would have been hit by a car. Or maybe just by receiving the help of a stranger, they had a brighter day and were full of warmth at their next human interaction.

These good deeds, one way or another, can have ramifications of the best kind, what Robert F. Kennedy once called "a tiny ripple of hope." I felt that so clearly the night of that charity event. *What can I do with the time that I have?* I thought. And so there I was, helping to raise money for the Red Cross, hoping that this deed would help someone in need, and send forth that tiny ripple to the next person, and so on down the line.

Star Trek did that for so many people. It is a documented fact that a great number of scientists, servicepeople, astronauts, and doctors went into those fields because they were inspired by what they saw on *Star Trek*. That has been one of its legacies. It gave people a voice; it sent a ripple through the television and touched millions of people. And not just by inspiring them to seek out new life-forms and new civilizations in their careers, but through its vision of a future in which humanity exists in a more harmonious fashion, where neither gender nor race nor any other number of differences stand in the way of people being able to live to their full potential.

When it comes to the question of *legacy,* all I know—all I *feel*—is that we should try to do good, try to remember the inherent connection we all have to each other, and to help nurture those connections.

If people still have questions for me after I'm gone, those strange advances of technology have offered me an opportunity to be able to continue to speak to those who want to hear from me. I recently worked with a company called StoryFile (which partnered with another company called PROTO) to create a 3D model of myself that can be projected as a hologram. Using a combination of holographic technology and artificial intelligence software, you will be able to press a button, and up I will pop, and you can ask me your questions. "Bill, what was it like growing up in Montreal?" And I will answer.

For five days, I fed information and answers into this technology. I only hope I answered enough questions that users won't be confronted with some version of "I don't know that one. Please try again." But gosh, isn't that something? I have remarked that you could put a holographic device on my gravestone, or perhaps somewhere less morbid. Theoretically, it could go anywhere, and there could be multiple versions, pop-ups all over the world. "Five years after his death, William Shatner is going on tour!" It's a funny idea, but each day, it becomes more and more plausible.

And yet the thought of returning to essential loneliness sits with me. On my album *Bill*, the song "Loneliness" ends with the line, "Aren't we always alone?" My hologram may answer questions for years to come, but will I have any answers when I'm gone?

I took a handful of violin lessons in my youth. Decades later, one of my granddaughters approached her mother one day, full of excitement. "I want to play the violin!" she bellowed. So, her mother dutifully arranged to get her child a violin and some lessons. And there was my granddaughter, full of exuberance, squeaking like a rusty swing as she attempted to convert her sudden passion for this instrument into a sound that didn't rival that of nails screeching down a chalkboard. Later, we were gathered for dinner, and someone put classical music on in the background.

"Oh!" my granddaughter cried, *"that's* the way it's supposed to sound." We all laughed and laughed. She gave up playing the violin shortly thereafter.

But I was struck by that sentence. "That's the way it's supposed to sound." The simple realization. Will each of us encounter a similar realization on our deathbeds, something like the realization of truths and the sound of a violin? "Oh, that's what family is." "Oh, that's what *love* is."

Over a quarter of a century ago, I said goodbye to my role as Captain Kirk in *Star Trek: Generations.* (Did you hear? A *bridge* fell on him.) As Captain Kirk passes on, he looks up, past the beautiful, reflective head of Captain Picard, and with quiet dignity exclaims, "Oh, my . . ."

How I wish I'd had a better take of that moment. The one that made it into the film feels full of dread. That *Oh, my* may as well be *Oh, shit.* What I really wanted to achieve in that moment was a feeling of wonder, much closer to

Oh, wow. Closer to *Oh, look at the glory of that!* and a little less *Oh, dear, here comes the man with the scythe.* I wanted it to feel like something astounding was taking place.

Famous psychologist and psychedelic drug advocate Timothy Leary is said to have remarked at the height of one of his acid trips, "Of course!" As if in one perfect moment (like when your dentist gives you nitrous oxide), he had all the answers. That is the moment I wanted for Captain Kirk, and I wonder with morbid fascination if I, William Shatner, have a similar moment waiting for me.

But not for a while. Right? Can you hear me, universe? I don't want to die!

In *Star Trek: Generations*, after Captain Kirk's exit from the canonical universe (those of you who have read my *Star Trek* novels will know that not even death could defeat old Captain James T.), Captain Picard remarks that we are all, in fact, mortal. Commander William Riker comes in with the rejoinder "I plan to live forever."

That is me. Death has never seemed to want a piece of me. The same way Captain Kirk solved the *Kobayashi Maru* test, I have kept cheating death. In all the movies I've made and stunts with which I've been involved, for some reason I've never gotten hurt, even if theoretically I should have. Even professional stuntmen aren't as lucky as I've been, and they race into danger and practice how to cheat death over and over and over again.

I was making a motorcycle movie near Lake Moses in northern Washington State. I have ridden motorcycles most of my life, and still do to this day. We had a stunt on a motorcycle, which required the rider to negotiate some sand dunes and then leap high off a dune. I was game to ride on the dunes, but leaping off the waves of the dunes was not something I had any experience with. "That's okay, Bill," they told me, amused that I was even considering offering to do the jump. "We have a stuntman for that."

My part of the stunt was to drive fast right up to the lip of the dune and then stop. We did that a bunch of times, then they reset for a shot of the jump. They positioned the cameras. They did all the safety checks. The stuntman revved up and took off! He went right up to the lip of the dune and made the jump. He went up into the air, he came down . . . and he fell off the motor-cycle.

We ran over to him as he lay there, in paralyzed agony. His girlfriend ran down to him. "Are you okay, honey?" The stuntman was in pain but tried to play it off like it was just another day at the office. His girlfriend then turned to me and said, "Mr. Shatner, could I have your autograph?" It was a light moment, but it was the last one for a while. We later learned that the stuntman had broken his back and would spend the rest of his life with paraplegia.

That could have been me. So many times, *it could have been me.* I've clung to the hood of a car going forty miles per hour, barely holding on as men with (fake) machine guns shot at me through the windshield. I've held on to the skids of a helicopter as it flew (attached by cables, but it's still terrifying). I have stood at the apex of a glacier, mere inches from a seemingly bottomless crevasse as cameras rolled, thinking to myself, *If I move even slightly, that will be the story of me.* "Actor William Shatner falls to death in icy crevasse. Film at eleven."

And yet, here I am. Alive and kicking. Well, kicking as much as I can.

In 2016, I had a major health scare. My doctors were convinced that I had an aggressive form of prostate cancer. In their view, I was a goner. I was stunned. I knew intellectually that the only constants in the world were death and taxes, and that like all others before me, I, too, would one day shuffle off this mortal coil and take my exit stage left (after paying my taxes). But in my heart, I couldn't accept it. How could I die when I had so much to live for?

A couple of lifestyle and supplement adjustments later, scans showed that my prostate was just fine. *What the hell?* Was there a smudge on the imaging equipment? One minute I was facing certain death, the next all was well.

After that apparent missed connection with the grimmest of reapers, I told folks that I had the answer to the question of how to live a long life. "Don't die," I declared. It's good advice, right? How can you argue with it? It is scientific fact that avoiding death leads to a longer life.

I have heretofore avoided death, and I think part of how I have done so is to keep discovering. Paul McCartney made an album some years ago he called *Memory Almost Full*. As a function of age, I cannot help but forget things as I go on. But I also learn things. If something falls out of my brain—a date, a quote, the exact detail of where I was and what I did on some particular day—it feels insignificant next to the power of what I am taking on. (Fortunately, I also have the aforementioned Kathleen Hayes, with her sharp memory and her internet computer phone devices to look things up for me.)

I am learning more each day. I am working on so many fronts. Thanks to the power of electronic books, I don't even have to go to the bookstore. If a book catches my eye, I can download it instantly and start reading it right there and then, while my passion for the subject consumes me. I read Robert Ballard's *Into the Deep: A Memoir from the Man Who Found* Titanic. I later interviewed him for a TV show. With a few clicks, I was able to call up all of Ballard's work and tear through it ahead of our interview. I am blessed to live in an age where technology makes that possible. I can do more, and in a shorter time frame, freeing up other hours to do more exploring. On the other hand, sometimes I can't get my iPhone camera to work, which I think is taking years off my life, so who knows.

But I'm hungry. I'm thirsty. I don't *have* to do any of these things. Not for any material reasons. I am taken care of financially. I am well-fed. (Too well-fed, frankly.) But as I get older, I find myself accessing an increasing urgency within me to absorb more. Earlier in my life, I found myself contemplating, as I'm sure we all have, *What the hell am I doing here? What does it all mean? Is it a cosmic joke?*

We try to give meaning to our lives through structure. You're born. You play with kids on the playground. You become a teenager, you have your Bar or Bat Mitzvah, your confirmation, your quinceañera. You graduate from high school or university and go out into the world. You get a job. You earn a living. You bring another child into the world. They begin the same cycle. But for what? For me, it is to keep my eyes open to the wonders of the universe. To smell those roses. To celebrate every moment of my existence by observing and taking in every moment of existence itself.

I was once quoted as saying, "Anything done well is an act of sex." I don't remember if those were my exact words, but that's how the quote read. What I was describing was an organic, loving feeling of excitement. Finding an answer, marking an achievement, feeling a sense of accomplishment. There are deeply religious people who have felt what they believe to be the "ecstasy of God." They feel a spirit move deep within them, and the expression of that feeling is an almost erotic explosion of enjoyment. I take pleasure in the acquisition of knowledge, and at times, there truly is an erotic energy to it. Sometimes you can bite into a piece of food . . . maybe you like fresh pineapple with a little bit of sriracha on it. You bite into it and you cannot help but moan and groan. "Oooh, ahhh, this is the most delicious thing I've ever tasted. Oh, my Lord!"

In my youth, I was a waiter at Montreal's Gibeau Orange Julep restaurant. Their signature drink is an orange juice mixed with sugar, milk, and egg whites. It sounds disgusting, but when people tasted it for the first time, you could see (and hear) the pleasure they experienced as it made its way down their throat. (I didn't see too much of it, as I was fired after tripping and dropping Orange Julep all over a customer. I guess Orange Julep helped make me an actor, as it was clear I wasn't much of a waiter.) That's what I meant by an act of sex. The pure erotic energy of that experience. And if you get it from spicy pineapple or the first gulp of an Orange Julep, more power to you. I got a similar feeling from some toasted rye bread once, so I can relate. If you can live your life in that manner, where you can attain those pure delights, I think you're doing something right.

For that, *quality of life* is important. I fear death. I fear a lot of things. I fear my dogs eating my furniture. (A friend of mine used hot sauce to quell his dogs' appetite for the stairs in his house—perhaps something I'll need to try if Espresso and Macchiato don't knock it off.) I also fear losing what keeps me alive long before my body expires. I fear incapacity. I am not alone in that, and yet I have learned that not everyone shares this fear. Fear of death is perhaps generic, but fear of incapacity may not be.

Some years ago, I had the privilege to interview a young Canadian actor, Kenneth Mitchell. Trekkers will know Kenneth from his appearances on *Star Trek: Discovery*. In 2018, Kenneth was diagnosed with amyotrophic lateral sclerosis, also known as ALS, or Lou Gehrig's disease, after the baseball player who was diagnosed with it in 1939. Lou Gehrig did not look at his condition with fear—at least not publicly. He wrote, "I intend to hold on as long as possible and then if the inevitable comes, I will accept it philosophically and hope for the best. That's all we can do."

In my talks with Kenneth Mitchell, I asked if he would be open to discussing what it is like to face his illness, and to eventually face death because of it. He said he'd be delighted to. He wanted to. And so, we talked. He wept about his children. Spending time with this vital young man, hearing him express his feelings on knowing that his body will continue to turn against him, was heartbreaking. The fact that he can face it with optimism is a testament to his bravery. He is a far braver man than I.

Other than Lou Gehrig, perhaps the most famous person to ever live with ALS was the late, great Professor Stephen Hawking. Hawking was a guest star on an episode of *Star Trek: The Next Generation* and had the unique distinction of being the only person to ever play himself on *Star Trek*. While working on the show, Hawking was given a tour of the engineering set. He looked at the warp core, where the dilithium crystals were glowing, and remarked, "I'm working on that." Years later, I went to several universities that were developing futuristic technologies and interviewed the professors and students and experts in those fields. Many of the technologies that seemed fictional back in those days have now come to fruition.

Decades later, I was fortunate to be able to interview Professor Hawking for a documentary I was making called *The Truth Is in the Stars*. When I had contacted him to ask if he would lend his expertise to the project, he agreed, but on the condition that he get to ask me something at the end of the interview. Naturally, I agreed.

I went to Cambridge and interviewed this brilliant man. As you know, Professor Hawking had long been unable to speak, and this was barely more than a year before he died. Slouched in his wheelchair in an angular fashion, he would twitch a muscle in his cheek, which was attached to a computer that would spell out what he was saying and relay it through a speaker. When it came to the questions I had wanted to ask for the book, I'd submitted them and he had answered them in advance, so he merely needed to hit the "speak" button and the mechanical voice of the computer would articulate his responses.

At the end of the interview, I returned to his request to ask *me* a question. He began spelling it out. It took a while, as he had to go one letter at a time. As he typed, I pondered what this pre-eminent mind of the twentieth century was going to ask me, a mere actor. My thoughts swelled with the possibilities; I hoped I'd be up to the challenge of giving an answer worthy of the man asking it.

After what seemed an eternity, Professor

Hawking finished his question and hit the "speak" button.

"Shatner. What was your favorite episode?"

I burst out laughing. Tears began to stream down my cheeks. *That* was his question. Bless him; he was a fan. I looked at him and could tell by the slight reddening of his cheeks that he was laughing, too. *I'd made Stephen Hawking laugh.* At first, I gave him the standard answer, which is Harlan Ellison's "City on the Edge of Forever," in which Kirk and Spock follow McCoy through the mysterious Guardian of Forever time portal to 1930s Earth to prevent the Federation's erasure from existence, and in which Kirk falls in love with social worker Edith Keeler (Joan Collins). It is a truly brilliant hour of television that deserves its place in the *Star Trek* pantheon. But then I went further: I think there are probably a dozen or so episodes that constitute the true wealth of science-fiction concepts and execution that *Star Trek* was able to give to the world.

A few that I recalled (although I had to research the titles later for this book) were "A Taste of Armageddon," in which the *Enterprise* visits a planet in which physical war has been replaced by a computer simulation that decided who lived and who died; "The Cage"/"The Menagerie," the original pilot and later two-part episode in which Captain Pike visits Talos IV and is subjected by the Talosians to captivity and mind games;

"Let That Be Your Last Battlefield," the famous episode about racial prejudice with two almost identical half-white, half-black races; "Journey to Babel," in which Spock must choose between his duty and saving his father's life; "The Trouble with Tribbles," for pure fun; "The Doomsday Machine," in which we see humankind wrestle with creating a weapon it can no longer control; "Mirror, Mirror," for conceptual brilliance; "The Devil in the Dark," for its meaningful take on the need for tolerance of all creatures; and finally "Amok Time," for its fascinating exploration of Vulcan culture.

Professor Hawking invited me to dinner at his home. This posed a bit of a dilemma for me. What do you do at dinner with a man who can't talk, who can't eat—at least, not in the same way most of us do? I did what I knew. I acted. I performed my one-man show for Stephen Hawking. Again, I got to see that rosy glow in his cheeks. It was marvelous. He had lived with his condition for so long that it was just a way of life for him; it wasn't scary. The same way Kenneth Mitchell looked positively toward the challenges ahead, and Lou Gehrig had stayed optimistic all those years before.

Perhaps it is because I have been fortunate enough to live such a full life for ninety-one years that I am so scared of losing it, and of losing the ability to function in the way to which

I am accustomed. I do not want to live past the point where my faculties fail me.

My father-in-law had Alzheimer's. He was entering the beginning of that part of his life and he knew it. He did not know what lay ahead. I asked if he would be willing to share his insights. He said he would, but how? "I'll buy you a voice-operated recorder," I told him. "When you think of it, you can just start talking and the recorder will capture all of it. What you're seeing, what you're thinking, what you're feeling. What are your fears? What are you dealing with as you head into the realms of where this disease may take you?" He was fearful but excited. We talked about turning it into a book, written from the firsthand perspective of someone tackling Alzheimer's. I bought him the recorder. The disease came on fast. When he remembered, he would speak into it, trying to extemporize his thoughts as they came to him.

A short while later, I visited him and picked up the recorder. Sadly, it was as he had feared. Most of it was nonsense. I don't mean that it was gibberish, but rather that he'd begin with thoughts about the struggle but then trail off into tangents, ultimately not reaching any conclusions. It was a very sad realization—the disease had robbed him of one of the most basic elements of his life: his thought process.

I had a fraction of an insight into Alzheimer's

once. I still ride horses competitively, but as I get older, I must ensure I can get my breath as we go through each routine. To do this, I need to stop longer between movements and hydrate to stave off the effects of the heat. One day, I was taking a breath between exercises, sitting on a chair, waiting for a horse to be brought up. I stood up quickly—too quickly—and I got vertigo. If you have ever experienced this—not just dizziness, but *real* vertigo—you know how frightening and disorienting it is. In a flash, you can be thrown to the ground by its nauseating effects. You don't know where you are. You don't know up and down. You lose contact with all reality.

I was lucky in that it had happened from the simple act of rising from a chair—I fell right back into the chair, and a few moments later, the dreadful sensation was gone, and I was myself again. But after seeing what had happened to my father-in-law, I thought, *Oh no, I wonder if this is what Alzheimer's is like.* Would it be like having vertigo? Where all of a sudden you don't know where you are, *who you are?* I do not want to encounter that moment in my life. I want to be shot dead before it happens. That's my fear talking, but it is so real to me, that fear.

In the late 1990s, I went to visit my friend DeForest Kelley, who had played Dr. McCoy on *Star Trek.* The Motion Picture & Television Fund runs a small but lovely hospital and assisted-living facility out in Woodland Hills, California. I had known "Dee" (as his friends called him) for over thirty years. He had been married to his lovely wife, Carolyn, for over fifty years. Dee had been diagnosed with stomach cancer and was living and receiving treatment at the hospital.

We had a wonderful catch-up and gabbed about the old days. As I was preparing to leave, Dee said, "You know Carolyn's here, right?" I hadn't been aware of that. His wife was living at the facility and had been diagnosed with Alzheimer's. I went over to the other wing and visited her. We got to talking and I said, "You know, Carolyn, this is a failing of mine, but in all the time we've known each other, I've neglected to ask where you were born."

Carolyn burst out in tears. "Please don't ask me that!" she cried. She couldn't remember where she was born. And she was so fearful of losing more. I understand that fear.

I hope to live the longest of lives. And at the end of my days, I want to be a tree.

What?

I wrote a song called "I Want to Be a Tree" for what I hope will be my next album. The lyrics are amusing so as to be entertaining, but the subject matter is real and meaningful to me. I have written about the interconnectedness of the world. I want to be a part of that symbiosis. In my will, I have made arrangements—and made it known to my children and my family—that when I die, I wish to be cremated and have my ashes put into a pod, which should then be deposited into the ground, with a tree planted over my remains. I want that tree to extract my goodness from the earth and grow from what I leave behind in the ground. I know where that tree will go in my backyard. I know the kind of tree. Every detail.

These are the lyrics to the song.

When my time has come
Don't put me in a box
And skip the fancy shiva
No platters of bagels and lox
Lay down that spike and chisel
No headstone will I need
Yeah when I die my wish is clear
Just plant me like a seed
'Cause I want to be a tree
Yes, I want to be a tree
With plenty of leaves and bark to spare
For everyone to see
I want to be a tree
Yes, I want to be a tree
You can sit right down under my shade
That'll be enough for me
I read it and it's true
Make a pod from my remains
Then stick me in the ground

And pray for sun and rain
The richness from my body
Will supercharge the earth
And like a natural maternity ward
To a sapling I'll give birth
So I want to be a tree
Yes, I want to be a tree
With plenty of leaves and bark to spare
For everyone to see
I want to be a tree
Yeah, I want to be a tree
You can sit right down under my shade
That'll be enough for me
So don't stick me in an urn
For some relative to keep
And please don't throw me overboard
To the bottom of the deep
No twenty-one-gun salute
So just put those guns to bed
I've got a much more peaceful wish
Bring the garden tools instead
'Cause I want to be a tree
Yeah, I want to be a tree
With plenty of leaves and bark to spare
For everyone to see
I want to be a tree
Yes, I want to be a tree
Standing, swaying firm and tall
Glorious and free
I want to be a tree

Yes, I want to be a tree
You can sit right down under my shade
That'll be enough for me
You can sit right down under my shade
That'll be enough for me

I want to be part of the planet, as it has been part of me, as it is part of all of us. That stardust that makes up every molecule. In the words of the Lakota, *Mitakuye Oyasin*: We are all related.

EPILOGUE

I have more to say. So much more. Can't stop, won't stop. To my last breath, I will grapple with knowing my race has not been completely run. The finish line is not of my choosing. There will always be more to experience, more to discover. More. *More.*

When I put together my album *Bill* with the inestimable Rob Sharenow and Dan Miller, as is customary we recorded more songs than would eventually make it onto the finished album. The songs on *Bill* are all of a theme, taken from stories of my life's journey; most of the additional songs were of a different theme: nature, connection, seeking out life's mysteries. In many ways, the thought process behind those songs inspired much of this book.

Rob, Dan, and I had hoped to turn this second set of songs into the basis of a new album (and by the time you read this, we may well have done so), but in the immediate future after *Bill*, a different opportunity arose.

During the writing of this book, in particular the "Listen to the Music" chapter, I sought out my friend Ben Folds for his wisdom. Ben and I reminisced and discussed the science, magic, and wonder of music—what it is, what it represents, what it makes us feel. Talking about our collaborations made us realize that we wanted to get together and make music once more.

In May 2017, Ben had been named the new artistic adviser to the National Symphony Orchestra, which performs most of its concerts at the hallowed Kennedy Center. Ben's task was to bring a new point of view and energy to the orchestra's programming, principally with the *Declassified* series. Because of COVID, the orchestra and its audience had been deprived of each other's company for two years, but it was announced that in April 2022, the series would recommence. Specifically, the Kennedy Center was planning several events focused on Earth Day. Ben asked, "Is that something that might interest you?"

"I'd be honored," I told him.

In my work with Rob Sharenow and Dan Miller, we'd had six songs in the repertoire that hadn't been selected for *Bill*. My discussions with Rob had plumbed the very depths of my feelings, producing poignant phrases, meaningful musings, and lyrics that captured the essence of the very subject that Ben had now asked me to perform: Earth, space, nature, exploration, and the fragile balance of it all.

Once again, I felt like I was being carried on a wave. Ben and I were vibrating together: Here we were, talking about a chapter of my new book, and at the same time, our goals and imaginations were aligning. He presented an opportunity to celebrate Earth Day through music, and I had songs on the very same subject matter that I was positively itching to perform.

We sent our song recordings to Ben, who assigned the orchestration to Jherek Bischoff, a phenomenal composer, arranger, producer, and performer. Jherek took five of our songs and set them to an orchestration played by more than sixty instruments. The sixth, "Are You the Bayou," was entrusted to our magnificent collaborator Dan Miller, who wrote a gorgeous, lush arrangement.

I was given a file with the orchestrations—played by computer synthesizers—and set to rehearsing.

Now, the most challenging part of the kind of music I perform is the absence of the natural ebbs and flows that one might expect with a verse-chorus-verse structure. In most songs with lyrics, there is a melodic line you can follow: "She loves you, yeah, yeah, yeah," "Happy birthday to you," "Row, row, row your boat," etc. You hear the music; you know where the lyrics fit in. If you come in a little too early or a little too late, you can easily catch up because that melodic line gives you signposts to follow.

With the orchestrations for my songs, which are spoken and not sung, there is no melody to follow. It is all mood and musical emphasis; no particular note or phrase I could hear would give me a clue that I was in the right place at the right time. For musicians like Ben Folds or the National Symphony, they know when to come in because they understand the underlying rhythm and tempo; and with a nod from the conductor, they know their cues exactly. I, on the other hand, had no such understanding. The best I could cling to was to try to remember a particular tinkling bell or the specific warble of a trumpet; even then, were I to get lost, I would have very little in the way of clues to guide me back to the path that kept words and music moving together correctly.

To say I was nervous would be an understatement. I was terrified. But also thrilled. The chance to perform never-before-heard songs that were of such import to me filled me with purpose. I rehearsed and rehearsed and rehearsed, probably more for this performance than for almost anything else in my career. I wanted so much to get it right. The lyrics were deeply meaningful to me because they were the embodiment of my personal experience. They were everything I had wanted to say and more, and my trip to outer space had only amplified their meaning. I was gripped by the spirit of what Martin Luther King Jr. memorably called "the fierce urgency of now."

I arrived in Washington two days before

the performance and had two rehearsals with the orchestra. The rehearsal process was that uncertainty I had feared writ large. I had no signposts. Where was I in the orchestrations? When did one phrase end and the next begin? If I thought of the orchestra as a marching band, I was out front, twirling a baton, unable to look behind me to see if the band was in lockstep with me or if I had wandered right off the path.

In addition to my six songs, there was also dialogue—a series of stories, introductions, and interstitial descriptions of the inspiration and meaning behind each piece. It was a lot to learn and I didn't want to mess it up, so I asked the Kennedy Center to provide a teleprompter. Unfortunately, they placed the monitor all the way at the back of the auditorium—far beyond the reach of my nonagenarian eyesight. They tried enlarging the font, but I could only see it if it displayed one word at a time. "The" "day" "I" "went"—it was an impossibility. "We'll move it closer to the stage and off to one side," they decided. That solved the eyesight problem, but now I found myself gazing mostly at one side of the audience. So I asked for monitors to be put up on either side of the stage, which enabled me, much like a politician giving a speech, to look in both directions and find the words without missing a beat.

The problem of timing remained: how to get

me on the same page as the orchestra. Someone suggested that Jherek, the orchestrator, could stand backstage with a camera on him, and they could put a small video monitor in front of me so he could direct me—give me signs on when to speed up, slow down, begin a verse, etc.

"If he's going to be in the auditorium," I said, "I don't want him on a TV screen—get him out here." So Jherek sat in the first row, in my lower peripheral vision. He gave me the signs, he *conducted* me, and it worked. We achieved unity with each other, and with the orchestra. We vibrated together. My fear left me. This was going to work. I could feel it.

When the night arrived, the concert hall was packed to capacity—some 2,400 seats. One night only. I began with an introduction I had written: "Music is everywhere." A blanket of silence settled over the hall. As an actor, you can feel when an audience member is listening, when they are leaning forward. It is as if we are connected by an umbilical cord, drawn to each other.

I've written and talked about the synchronicity of the universe; how things just seem to connect us to one another. I believe part of what makes that possible is the desire to reach out and grab that connection. No one knows quite how or why, but every so often, whether it's through prayer or contemplation, meditation or awareness, or even just the suggestive power of our imaginations, sometimes we tap into something. A rhythm, a vibration, a perfect moment where it all comes together. All my anxiety had disappeared during rehearsals as each person involved came together with everyone else in unity of purpose. From the incredible musicians to Ben and his artistic vision, from the gentleman positioning the monitors to Jherek finding the perfect spot from which to communicate the musical flow to me, it all came together.

And it had to be live. We had to all experience it together in one place, one moment in time.

In a recording studio, you can change things, you can correct mistakes. You can layer in additional tracks, and record multiple takes and choose the best of the bunch.

We had no such options. To do this kind of show live was to tremble on the edge of disaster.

In a scene from *Amadeus*, my young coauthor's favorite movie (and one of mine, too), composer Antonio Salieri scrutinizes several pieces of Mozart's work, recognizing with jealousy the utter perfection that presented itself on the page: "Displace one note, and there would be diminishment. Displace one phrase, and the structure would fall."

While I am no Mozart, that quote reflects how I felt about all the people functioning in harmony around me, and my place in that harmony with them. It could have been a catastrophe. And yet, somehow, that was never going to happen. The universe was taking care of me. I would not fall. Everything would happen as it was supposed to, and it would be live for all of us in that room to feel.

After the show, the audience stood in sustained, captivated applause, cheering us back onto the stage three times—just bows and words of gratitude, since we didn't have any additional songs to play for an encore. Backstage after our final bow, musicians, friends, and the Kennedy Center folks streamed into my dressing room, grinning from ear to ear, so delighted to have been part of this night. We celebrated together, taking pictures, sharing laughs, and later partying the night away at the nearby Watergate Hotel.

There was something about this experience— it was the culmination of everything I have tried to express in these pages. The ultimate feeling of connection. From the moment I uttered those words, "Music is everywhere," the audience and I were as one. Music is *vibration,* and we were vibrating together on the same wavelength. That could not have happened with an album.

My quest to express myself through music has been a learning process, and it was only on *Bill* that I felt I'd finally arrived at my destiny. This live performance was the apex of that arrival; the peak of the mountaintop.

What made it ever so special were the journeys

I had taken to get there. Not just musical ones, with my first album tanking yet finding its way to a young boy at a North Carolina yard sale, but my journeys across this Earth, and then out of it. I had gone to space. I had seen the tiny blue marble, had witnessed the treacherously delicate balance between life and nothingness, and had returned to tell the tale of what I thought we needed to do to save that balance.

We played "I Want to Be a Tree," a love song I'd written for my family to reassure them that I will be all around them in nature when my physical presence is gone. And we closed with the song I so desperately needed to write after I had come back from space. It is called "So Fragile, So Blue," and is as much a chronicle of my journey to the final frontier as it is an exhortation to cherish this planet of ours and to save it—and ourselves—before it's too late. The orchestra began with Alexander Courage's familiar *Star Trek* theme, and I launched myself with every fiber of my being into the lyrics.

The song is structured in four parts: Lifting Off, Space, The Blue Dot, and finally, Touching Down. As the orchestra surged behind me, I could feel the urgency—that fierce urgency—pouring out of me. With each refrain of the chorus, I implored in the throes of desperation, *"So fragile, so blue . . . what can we do? What can we DO?"*

I arrived at the final verse—the elucidation of my journey home. From a wellspring of ninety-one years of human emotion and experience, I announced,

When I finally touched down
Finding my feet on solid ground
A feeling so profound
That I'd never had

No triumph or joy
Not like a little boy
Who had finally played with a toy
I felt deeply, deeply sad

A sadness so real and so deep
That I might never sleep
But I just have to keep
And let people know

Boldly go
Boldly go
Boldly go

Boldly go means to love
To take responsibility of
What's below and above
And never live to regret

I hope I never recover
From what I discovered

Like a long-lost lover
I had left to neglect

Mountains, trees, birds, beasts
Life-giving water, magnificent feasts
North, south, west, east
All human reactions from terror to fun
All that breathes, swims, flies, or runs
Literally everything under the sun

Every ant that crawls
Every ocean squall
Snails, lions, sand,
The tiniest creatures we don't under-
    stand

Redwoods touching the sky
A cat's glassy eyes
The plains waving grass
The miracle of glass

A beautiful child
Gray wolves running wild
Every smell fine or foul
Every howl, song, or growl

The fire, wind, and rain
Purest pleasure, piercing pain
The heat of our skin
All original sin

Bound up together
Built to last forever
Connected as one
But coming undone
It's all ours to lose
A fate that we choose

So fragile, so blue
What can we do?
So fragile, so blue
What can we do?
What can we do?
What can we do?

A day or two after the show, I was asked whether I would consider taking this performance on the road, or at least arrange a second show to share this feeling with more people. We had captured the concert on seventeen cameras and dozens of microphones, so I knew it would live on and be available to those who couldn't be there in Washington, and I also knew I didn't want to attempt a repeat performance. For me, it was a singular moment, and I will forever be fulfilled by what I felt that night. The magic of that universal unity.

It was the ultimate expression of my life's journey. I have lived a thousand lives, I have journeyed far and wide . . . I have gone boldly, carried on by a river of fate, to a destination I cannot see, but to which each day I am brought one step closer. I have searched my whole life for meaning, for connection, and though I cannot touch its essence or unravel its vast mystery, I believe that in my soul, I have found what I have been looking for.

ACKNOWLEDGMENTS

Josh Brandon is a wonderful artist. He is adept at many things and, as you can see, he has a marvelous facility with words. I also want to acknowledge two friends, Robert Sharenow and Daniel Miller, whose contribution to the poetry of our albums, some of which are quoted in this book, is more than graceful. And thanks to Kathleen Hayes. Her exact title is difficult to come by—she is less than a partner and more than an assistant—but she is completely wonderful.

—William Shatner

I would like to thank my parents, Sid and Julie, who believed in and encouraged me when I opted for a career in the dreaded entertainment industry.

To my wonderful long-suffering literary agent, Vanessa Livingston; my terrific book agent, Victoria Sanders; and our irreplaceable editor, Benee Knauer—thank you from the bottom of my heart for your incredible vision and guidance.

I am in great debt to the unflappable Kathleen Hayes for her patience and encyclopedic mind, to the ball of sunshine that is my assistant Katie Pierce, and to marvelous Anna Scantlin and

Morgan Ecker for transcribing the many hours of interviews and discussions that went into this book.

I am beyond grateful to the one and only Bill Shatner, without a doubt the most interesting person I have ever met, and a man who has probably forgotten more about every subject in the world than I will ever know. Bill, thank you for your kindness, for believing in me, and for saying "yes."

Finally, to my darling wife, Elizabeth: you are my absolute everything. Thank you for being born, and for charting a path right to my heart.

—Joshua Brandon

Center Point Large Print
600 Brooks Road / PO Box 1
Thorndike, ME 04986-0001 USA

(207) 568-3717

US & Canada:
1 800 929-9108
www.centerpointlargeprint.com